Vygotsky's Psychology-Philosophy

A Metaphor for Language Theory and Learning

COGNITION AND LANGUAGE
A Series in Psycholinguistics • Series Editor: R. W. RIEBER

A Continuation Order Plan is available for this series. A continuation order will bring delivery of each
new volume immediately upon publication. Volumes are billed only upon actual shipment. For further
information please contact the publisher.

University of Stirling Library, FK9 4LA
Tel. 01786 - 467220

POPULAR LOAN

This item is likely to be in heavy demand.
Please RETURN or RENEW no later
than the last date stamped below.

– 2 DEC 2002		

Vygotsky's Psychology-Philosophy

A Metaphor for Language Theory and Learning

Dorothy Robbins

Central Missouri State University
Warrensburg, Missouri

Kluwer Academic / Plenum Publishers
New York, Boston, Dordrecht, London, Moscow

Library of Congress Cataloging-in-Publication Data

Robbins, Dorothy
    Vygotsky's psychology-philosophy: a metaphor for language theory and learning/
Dorothy Robbins.
        p. cm. — (Cognition and language)
    Includes bibliographical references and indexes.
    ISBN 0-306-46423-3
        1. Vygotsky, L. S. (Lev Semenovich), 1896–1934. 2. Psychology—Soviet
Union—History. I. Title. II. Series.

    BF109.V95 R63 2000
    150'.92—dc21

                                                                            00-034937

ISBN: 0-306-46423-3

© 2001 Kluwer Academic / Plenum Publishers, New York
233 Spring Street, New York, N.Y. 10013

http://www.wkap.nl/

10 9 8 7 6 5 4 3 2 1

L. S. Vygotsky
(Photo courtesy of A. A. Leontiev.)

Foreword

You hold in your hands a new book. Professor Dorothy Robbins dedicated it to one of the aspects of the cultural heritage of the famous psychologist L. S. Vygotsky. His activity (*deyatelnost*) was multifaceted. He had input into different fields of psychology: its methodology, psychology of art, pathopsychology, the psychology of child and adolescent development, pedagogical psychology, general psychology, speech psychology, and other fields. Within his various activities he enriched not only psychology, but a variety of different sciences/academics—pedagogics, defectology, psychiatry, literary critical theory, and linguistics. Some famous scientists feel that he left his mark in fields of various scientific areas that did not exist during his lifetime—such as psycholinguistics, semiotics, and cybernetics.

Many psychologists and linguists conduct research in the spirit of his ideas that are contained within his approach of cultural–historical theory of human psychological development, all created by Vygotsky as early as the 1920s and 1930s; these ideas have become popular among scientists in different countries in the last decades. The use of Vygotsky's theories, even beyond the frame of psychology, turns out to be fruitful. I hope that this new book by Dorothy Robbins will help readers understand the deeper meaning of the scientific/academic research undertaken by my father and the scientific results that were obtained by him.

Gita L'vovna Vygodskaya
Moscow, Russia

Preface

This volume is an introduction to L. S. Vygotsky and his theories of language—all of which relate to Chomsky—and second language acquisition (SLA). Vygotsky's psychology–philosophy within this framework should be understood as a *metatheory* and as a metaphor. It is hoped that more thought will be given to a genetic–developmental (e.g., genetic referring to the starting point) approach in both the research and pedagogy of theories of language, viewing all learners within the understanding of their *potentiality*. This approach is not *modal*, nor a *method*. It is assumed that practitioners and researchers should be engaged in a personal struggle to establish an individual framework of theory and pedagogy, hence there is no universal answer given to the learning of language.

The central tenets of Vygotskian *history as change*, together with the use of *dialectics* to overcome *dualisms*, are placed within a higher level of Spinozian monism. It is with this understanding that Vygotsky was a man interested in *synthesis*, not only *thesis* and *antithesis*. The thoughts offered in this volume are an attempt to present Vygotsky's thinking in much of its entirety (excluding "defectology" and "paedology"). For this purpose many quotations have been included so that readers may refer to the original works in translation.

The basic focus of this volume revolves around an understanding of the *cultural–historical* perspective that Vygotsky adopted, which was semiotic in nature. In many respects this approach stands in direct opposition to the *socio-cultural* heritage that is more prevalent in the West. In this book *thought* is the focus of study as it is related to action, with the individual as an active agent still being placed at the heart of all arguments. The focus on *thought* stands in contrast to *sociocultural* theory that takes action (activity), not thought, as its focus. There should be no confusion regarding the fact that both theories view the individual as an active agent. Semiotic mediation is a key to many of the issues raised here, in particular the concept of *self-regulation.*

After summarizing the main points of Vygotsky's psychology–philosophy, there is a comparison of Vygotskian theories of language to the philosophical side of Chomskyan linguistics. However, in reality, the theories of these two men cannot be directly compared since they deal with different dimensions of reality (e.g., one with real time in an educational setting, the other with idealized time and idealized speaker-hearers). The next focus relates more directly to the field of second language acquisition (SLA) and applied linguistics, including a discussion of universal grammar (UG). The concluding chapter examines the Vygotskian psychological understanding of grammar, leading into thoughts on functional grammar.

Many writers in America and parts of Europe attempt to place Vygotsky's thoughts within a Marxist philosophical tradition. However, the highest level of understanding of various authors remains within the level of *dialectics*, rarely placing dialectics within a yet higher position of Spinozian monism. The aspect of monism is often misunderstood as determinism; however, from the Spinozian point of view, monism is not a static concept isolated from the effects of dialectics. This is a most difficult model to understand from a Western–Cartesian perspective, because on the surface it runs counter to human free will. However, individual freedom is to be found within a Spinozian higher level of understanding, not just within the choice that each individual makes separated from the whole. Seldom do authors in the West use Marx's understanding of "cell" as a holistic point of reference, remaining within the dualistic system that Vygotsky himself tried to overcome. The result is that many theorists assume that the *lower mental processes* and *higher mental processes* do not form a continuum. However, after a closer reading of Vygotsky's intentions, it is claimed that with different genetic roots—different trajectories of development and regression—there is indeed one continuum, not to be understood as one line of development. The analogy is given of the earth as a planet sustaining many different life forms, with the earth representing one continuum. This theory is not meant to be understood as being linear but rather represents an asymmetrical dialectic within the dynamic circle of Spinozian monism.

We are now in a post-Chomskyan and pre-Vygotskian era regarding future theories of language. Chomsky's linguistic theories coincided with many political realities of the United States from the 1950s through the 1990s emerging from the thinking of *behaviorism* (in psychology, linguistics, and politics). Chomsky represents the individual, one who is independent of a social setting, and he is perhaps the John Wayne of American abstract thinking—or better, he has been labeled the Picasso of linguistics. Vygotsky represents the connectedness of the individual to society (and vice versa), the dialectics of change, and the potentiality of the individual personality. The irony between Chomsky and Vygotsky is that Chomsky (writing within an individualistic system) offers nothing in terms of guidelines for individual growth, where all are supposed to be equal (under the guise of the ideal speaker-hearer who always represents the majority), whereas Vygotsky firmly believed in the tenets of a socialist future of education within the philosophy of Marx, yet his theories were designed (and are now being practiced by his granddaughter and her family) for the individual within society. Vygotsky's theories have lasted many years after his death, and promise to become a vital, dynamic basis of education, as well as to offer a new psychological focus in language theory for the future. Many writers have stated that he was so futuristic that we will only understand his thoughts when we are well into the twenty-first century. It is my hope that the futuristic thinking of Vygotsky will last for a long time to come. I would like to thank Eliot Werner, Robert W. Rieber, Adan Cohen, and Brian Halm for their untiring support of this project, and for their kindness and generosity.

This book is dedicated to the memory of L. S. Vygotsky and his wife Rosa, whose lives were a tribute to setting standards of excellence, and ultimately to living by those high standards during very difficult times. It is also dedicated to Gita L'vovna, Elena, Gennadi, Lev, Alexei, and Oleg, as well as to Tamara Lifonova, Vladimir Spiridonov, Elena Berejikovskaya, Inna, Anna, and Ksusha—all of whom are carrying on a living legacy of Vygotsky filled with pride, dignity, excellence, laughter, innovation, humility, joy, and love.

Dorothy Robbins

Contents

Vygotsky's Psychology-Philosophy
A Metaphor for Language Theory and Learning

I have forgotten the
word I wished to say, and my thought, unembodied,
returns to the realm of shadows

I forgot the word that I wanted to say,
And thought, unembodied, returns
to the hall of shadows

I forgot the word
which I wanted to say, and the thought,
lacking material form, will return to
the chamber of shadows

I wanted to utter a word, but that word
I cannot remember; and the bodiless thought
will now return to the palace of shadows

The word I forgot
Which Once I wished to say
and voiceless thought
Returns to shadows' chamber

(*The Swallow* by Osip Mandelstam)[1]

---

[1]These translations of Mandelstam's poem "The Swallow" were taken in the following order: (1) L. S. Vygotsky (1962). *Thought and Language*. Editors and translators, Hanfmann and Vakar. (2) L. S. Vygotsky (1978). *Collected works of L. S. Vygotsky*. Vol. 1. Editor R. Rieber (3) A. N. Leontiev (1978). *Activity, consciousness, and personality*. (4) L. S. Vigotsky (1961). *Thought and speech* in Saporta. (5) L. S. Vygotsky (1994a). *Thought and language*. Editor Alex Kouzlin.

Background Information on Vygotskian Theory and Vygotsky the Man

INTRODUCTION

Reading various translations of the poem by Mandelstam offers a multitude of interpretations of the Russian original, each contributing a different nuance. The same is true for any interpretation of the writings of L. S. Vygotsky, leaving one to wonder where to begin a method of analysis. For example, Davydov and Radzikhovskii stated that:

> Like all cultural phenomena, Vygotsky's work is not amenable to being studied outside of its historical context . . . But it is possible to outline a two fold approach to the study of his ideas by taking the historical context into account. One can begin with the contemporary state of science and attempt to identify aspects of Vygotsky's approach that do or do not share similarities with various theories. . . . one can then express a preference for one or another alternative. . . . But a second approach is also possible. . . . It is possible to evaluate Vygotsky's works on the basis of their internal logic. (Davydov & Radzikhovskii, 1985, pp. 36–37)

Throughout all of the chapters emphasis is placed on a *cultural–historical* approach (including "genetic–developmental" origins) instead of a *sociocultural* or activity theory approach. The basic difference revolves around a focus on *internal structures* (e.g., semiotics of "thought," *the unconscious as the seat of creativity*, aesthetics, etc.) as opposed to a focus on *external structures* (e.g., action). In North America the predominant focus on the *sociocultural* aspect of Vygotskian theory was primarily adopted by James Wertsch[2] (and he was greatly

[2]James Wertsch stated: "I use the term *sociocultural* because I want to understand how mental action is situated in cultural, historical, and institutional settings. I have chosen this term rather than others

influenced by the tenets of Russian activity theory), which best represent his research interest in *tool-mediated action*. However, the approach taken here is based on the description of cultural–historical psychology compared with activity theory as described by V. P. Zinchenko:

> The main difference is that for cultural–historical psychology, the central problem was and remains the mediation of mind and consciousness. For the psychological theory of activity, the central problem was object-orientedness, in both external and internal mental activity. Of course, in the psychological theory of activity the issue of mediation also emerged, but while for Vygotsky consciousness was mediated by culture, for Leont'ev [Leontiev] mind and consciousness were mediated by tools and objects. (Wertsch et al., 1995, p. 41)

During the 1930s the followers of Vygotsky rejected *semiotic mediation* as an overarching principle of *activity theory*, placing *practical actions* at the center of their research.[3] For this reason the term *cultural–historical* is used throughout this volume (instead of *sociocultural*) to situate the understanding of Vygotsky within a European (German and Spinozian) philosophical–historical–Marxist framework.

The attempt here is not to side with any theorist, nor to exclude any theorist, but to take an ethnomethodological stance in understanding the Vygotskian approach from the Russian semiotic perspective as much as possible.[4] When trying to stand back and view Vygotsky in his own setting, which is an exercise in speculation only, it should be remembered that the Russian mentality is different from that in the West. The point of explanation that is used here is the concept of "self" and "I" in the Russian language. An example is that

> ... there is no noun in the Russian language that is equivalent to the English word, *self*. There does exist a pronoun "-self" that is used in combinations such as "myself" (ya sam), "herself" (ona sama), "self-control," "self-analysis," or "self-consciousness." In Orthodox Russian the term *self (sam)* existed as a noun standing for the head of a household ... (Koltsova et al., 1996, p. 115)

In understanding the Russian intellectual mentality of the 1920s it might be paradoxical for some readers to discover that Germany played a major role in influencing the philosophical–psychological stance of many thinkers.

... in order to recognize the important contributions of several disciplines and schools of thought to the study of mediated action. On the one hand, I wish to recognize the contributions made by Vygotsky and his colleagues. . . . On the other, I wish to recognize the contributions made by many contemporary scholars of culture. . . . A term such as *sociohistorical–cultural* would be more accurate, but it is obviously too cumbersome" (Wertsch, 1991, p. 16). For further discussion, see James Wertsch et al. (1995, pp. 3–10).

[3]See Kozulin (1986, p. 272).

[4]Jacques Haenen stated that "according to him [James Wertsch], we should be talking about something like a Vygotskian approach rather than a Vygotskian theory, because the latter, in any strict sense, does not exist" (Haenen, 1995, p. 103).

Additionally, most of the Russian intellectuals during that period were fluent in German, with some scholars having studied in Germany.[5] Many of the Russian scholars wrote in German and in international journals, such as the *Journal of Genetic Psychology*. For example, in 1929, the editorial board of this journal was made up of people such as Charlotte Bühler, Ed. Claparède, I. P. Pavlov, William Stern, E. L. Thorndike, John B. Watson, and A. R. Luria. It is no secret that many of Vygotsky's ideas were not original with credit always being given to the appropriate sources. When viewing articles in the *Journal of Genetic Psychology* from the 1920s it is easy to see to what degree Vygotsky was probably influenced. He himself had an article in the 1929, Vol. XXXVI: 415–434, titled *"The Problem of the Cultural Development of the Child."* In the same journal there are two articles by Dorothea McCarthy, to whom Vygotsky gave partial credit for his understanding of the *Zone of Proximal Development*.[6]

When attempting to understand Vygotsky it is important to realize that the classical influence of Descartes was not present in Russia to the same extent as in the West. It was A. A. Potebnya (1835–1891), hardly known in the West, who brought back the ideas of Wilhelm von Humboldt (a German) to Russia. Humboldt was most influential at the very core of European intellectual thinking at the turn of the century. In order to grasp the ideas put forth by Humboldt, a longer quote is offered:

> In the age of the growing influence of the positivist world-view, Potebnya brought the philological and humanistic ideas of the great German thinker Wilhelm von Humboldt to Russia. It was in Potebnya's book that Vygotsky first confronted the mystery of the relationship between language and thought. Their relationship is traditionally conceived of in three alternatives: (a) thought coincides with language, (b) language serves as an external envelope of thought, and (c) thought achieves its becoming in language. Humboldt, and Potebnya after him, developed this latter alternative, and convincingly showed that nothing warrants the original identification of thought with language. Nonverbal thought is as real as preintellectual speech. For example, there is a nonverbal, puzzle-solving type of intellect, and preintellectual, emotive. At the same time

---

[5]"Historically, Russian intellectual life has been most closely connected with that of Germany (see Joravsky, 1989; Valsiner, 1988). In the pre-1917 period, many Russian scientists received their education in Germany, and published in German-language journals. This tendency continued in the 1920s but was ended in the early 1930s by the advent to power of radical tendencies in both the Soviet Union and Germany. Most of the psychologists in the 1920s were fluent in German, able to both read and write in the language" (van der Veer & Valsiner, 1991, p. 156).

[6]Since many theorists will be mentioned from whom Vygotsky borrowed directly or indirectly, Dorothea McCarthy will be used as a special example, with her 1930 book *The language development of the preschool child*. She spoke about the meaning of speech for the child offering stages of development, then discussing imitation, the first word, gestures, sentence formation, and so on. In short, it is much easier to see that although Vygotsky criticized the eclectic method in general, many of his ideas were adopted from others during this period of time. This comment is not made to diminish the accomplishments of Vygotsky, but to show the importance of other ideas of scholars who have been forgotten, or who are not as well known.

Humboldt and Potebnya refused to accept the idea of language's externality with respect to thought. Conceptual content is in no way independent of its linguistic form. To clarify this point Humboldt introduced a potent concept of the "inner form" of language. The existence of the inner form of a word is clearly felt by any translator struggling to render a certain concept in another language . . . The importance of the inner form of language for thought resulted in the different language-based world outlooks (*sprachliche Weltansicht*) of different peoples. Comparative linguistics is therefore not just a science of different linguistic structures, but also a science of how people refract reality through the prism of their language. According to Humboldt, language is a world of its own (*wahre Welt*) which mediates the world of objective phenomena and the inner world of man . . . Potebnya also pointed to the inherent ambivalence of language, which is objective as a common property of a given liguistic group and yet is subjective in the speech of each individual . . . the same ambivalence reveals itself in the duality of expression versus comprehension. What is said never coincides with what is comprehended . . . Finally, it is important to note that Humboldt defined language as *activity (Tätigkeit)*, rather than as a finished structure. Language is not a finished thing, but a creative process; it is not "ergon" but "energeia." (Kozulin, 1990, pp. 19–20)

Hypothesis: *In relating Vygotsky to Western humanities, it will be virtually impossible to understand the Russian background by placing the overall philosophical context within the Western philosophy of Descartes. One starting point for understanding Vygotsky is not Descartes, but Wilhelm von Humboldt.*

Many of the points made by Humboldt were criticized by Potebnya, with Vygotsky then criticizing aspects of Potebnya; for example, Potebnya's lack of use of semiotic devices in understanding art, as well as his narrow focus on the image of the general psychological impact of texts.[7] Humboldt was a defender of a type of linguistic relativity, later to be taken up and interpreted somewhat differently by Sapir and Whorf, and it was at this juncture that Vygotsky developed his ideas regarding thought and speech.[8]

The following section offers background information on various theories of Lev Vygotsky, including stories about his life in general. There is a review of possible misunderstandings generated from Russian theories that have similar terminology in the West but different meanings. It is hoped that when reading Vygotsky the Russian cultural background will be used as a filter in better understanding and synthesizing the material offered. It should be remembered that Vygotsky's name is spelled differently in various transliterations; for example, one can find Vygotski, Vygotskii, Vygotskij, Wygotski, Vigotski, or Vigotsky. The

---

[7]Cf. Wertsch (1985b, p. 84).

[8]For more information on Humboldt and Potebnya, check the following references: (1) Daniels (1993b, p. 24): "So, Vygotsky transforms Von Humboldt's emphasis on the word's inner form into a site in which the interaction between language and thought can be studied." (2) Innis (1982, pp. 82–84). (3) Blanck (1992). (4) L. S. Vygotsky (1971, pp. 90–91) *in The Psychology of Art.* (5) R. van der Veer (1997, Vol. 3, p. 7). (5) A. R. Luria (1979), p. 205), *The making of mind.* (6) L. S. Vigtosky [Vygotsky] (1961, p. 517).

same differences of spelling also apply to the names Luria (Lurya, Luriya), and Leontiev (Leontyev, Leont'yev, Leont'ev).

The following section provides an overview of some misunderstandings that can occur in extrapolating a Russian background on to a Western–Cartesian understanding of theory.

Caveats in Terminology—Problems between Vygotskian and Cartesian Thinking

A. Marxism.   The problem begins with many interpreters of Vygotsky writing about certain elements that fit the understanding of each individual author. It is interesting, for example, that Kozulin has not included an understanding of Vygotsky as a classical Marxist, whereas Yaroshevsky has tried to construct Vygotsky within a modern Marxist psychology. The entire aspect of Marxism has remained sensitive in the West with the 1966 translation of *Thought and Language* only taking up 153 pages, whereas the Russian original had 318 pages, where many quotes referring to Marxism were omitted for Western readers.[9] Vygotsky was certainly a philosophical Marxist interested in helping create a Marxist society from his understanding, which might be called a utopian society today. Professors Davydov & Zinchenko (1989) have maintained that for ". . . Vygotsky, Marxist philosophy was not a dogma or a theory in which one could find the answers to all the concrete questions of psychology" (p. 28).

It is hypothesized that within Cartesian thinking Hegel's *dialectic* is hardly understood and is often disassociated from the Marxist heritage that came later. Vygotsky's concept of the dialectic was more in line with classical Marxist philosophy using the dialectic primarily as a heuristic in order to activate a *dynamic* sense of change primarily within an educational (not philosophically abstract) framework. It is further hypothesized that without a Marxist understanding of the dialectic, Vygotskian theories relating to *history as change* and the *law of general genetic development*, as well as *internalization* cannot be understood in their entirety.

B. Behaviorism–Neobehaviorism.   In the early stages of Vygotsky's career the distinction between *lower mental processes* (which are innate) and *higher mental processes* (which are cultural) were not explained clearly. Therefore, misunderstandings regarding Vygotsky's approach have followed with various criticisms sometimes assuming the label *(neo) behaviorism*. A typical example of possible confusion can be found with phrases such as *consciousness*

[9]Kozulin (1994, p. 116).

being the "reflex of reflexes," which Vygotsky later changed. This type of early terminology led to assumptions about Vygotsky representing behaviorism, even within the area of consciousness. The next quote explains some of this confusion in the following way:

> Vygotsky . . . objected to the contention that human behavior is simply a sum of reflexes. "It is true," he wrote, "that the reflex is the foundation, but from it you can learn nothing about the building which will be constructed" (p. 181). While admitting that sensations, speech, instincts and emotions are reflexes, he nonetheless maintained that when the concept of reflex was given a universal meaning, it lost its psychological significance. At this point, however, Vygotskii [Vygotsky] was still close to behaviorism. . . . (Rahmani, 1973, p. 39)

Michael Cole, who is responsible for introducing many of Vygotsky's ideas to the West also had problems in understanding Vygotsky's position on behaviorism from the vantage point of American psychology. He stated that

> initially I interpreted cultural–historical psychology as the rough equivalent to American neobehaviorism of the 1960s. Vygotsky diagrammed the "cultural habit of behavior" using a "mediated stimulus–response" formulation (S–x–R) that looked uncannily like the diagrams drawn by the students of well-known learning theorists such as Clark Hull and Kenneth Spence, who had great influence on the way general psychology approached the study of cognitive development . . . I didn't pay this discussion much mind; I was working with rats and adults to discover universal laws of learning, not with children in cultural contexts. (Cole, 1996, p. 105)

Much of the irony of this interpretation is the fact that Russian psychology has viewed American behaviorism as placing the individual in a passive state of being, monitoring $S \Rightarrow R$ responses of particular individuals in experiments. In 1973, A. A. Leontiev [Leont'ev] criticized this approach as follows:

> A particularly widespread theory (especially in the United States) is the behaviorist view, which postulates that not only trivial acts of verbal behavior (such as "Hi!"–"Hi!") but also the most complex speech acts can be reduced to elementary reflex responses to verbal or nonverbal stimuli. The behaviorist view of verbal behavior, both for methodological and for purely psychological considerations, is unacceptable to us. (A. A. Leont'ev, 1973, p. 24)[10]

Vygotsky considered the lower mental processes to be innate and passive and in many respects it is ironic that this is the level at which many Russian scholars in psycholinguistics have viewed much of contemporary American linguistic research.[11] It is an interesting paradox in the sense that North Americans view

---

[10]Another statement referring to Russian criticisms of American psychology was from J. Wertsch (1981, p. 22): "Furthermore, Soviet psychologists often criticize American empirical studies on the grounds that experimental conditions create a situation in which the goals involved are so artificial that the data about the subjects' performance can tell us nothing about psychological processes carried out under natural conditions."

[11]"To sum up those features of Soviet psychology which distinguish it most from its Anglo-Saxen counterpart, the former emphasizes the *active* part played by the subject (and especially the conscious

themselves, on the whole, as being active individuals with an active research agenda in linguistics, even though the underlying tenets of innatism represent Chomskyan linguistic determinism, whether willingly or not. On the other hand, many North American psychologists and linguists have generally interpreted their Russian counterparts as focusing on socialization and not on the *individual* per se, nor on the *personality formation of the individual*, which was Vygotsky's over-arching goal. David Bakhurst (1986) has explained Vygotsky's position in the following way:

> "Socialisation," the all-pervading influence of the community upon the child, is not to be conceived as that which in principle *limits* individuality, but as that which makes possible the child's emergence as a self-determining subject. Vygotsky's position represents a theory of the *social genesis of the self.* (p. 117)

What comes to many as a surprise is that

> in ideological declarations Soviet psychology is both Marxist and Pavlovian, and largely indifferent to the illogic of the combination. In concrete research and teaching, Soviet psychology is neither Marxist nor Pavlovian, and never has been. The most important Soviet psychologists have formed a school of cognitive studies very much like Piaget's, though few of them have been willing to acknowledge the affinity. (Joravsky, 1987, p. 189)

Vygotsky's psychology–philosophy clearly differs from the traditional approach to Russian psychological theory. For example, Peeter Tulviste (1989a, p. 37) wrote that Vygotsky's views are now being seen as an alternative to behaviorism and to Piaget. It is important to understand that Vygotsky did not try to exclude behaviorism from his overall psychology–philosophy; however, it was firmly positioned within the lower mental processes, which should not be confused with the higher mental processes.

Since Vygotsky's psychology–philosophy contained *one* continuum including the *lower mental processes* (i.e., direct perception, involuntary memory, preverbal thinking) occupying the lower end of the scale, misunderstandings and behaviorist assumptions have been common from a Cartesian–Western perspective. In general, thinkers within the Cartesian model of duality have traditionally understood that there are two distinct processes of lower and higher mental capacities that do not form one continuum for Vygotsky, primarily because of the break with the lower mental processes via sign mediation. However, within the Spinozian model of understanding, one continuum of lower and higher mental processes does not exclude varying *attributes* with distinct lines of origin and different trajectories of development.

---

human subject) in *structuring* his own environment and his own experience, in contrast to the traditional (though perhaps weakening) Anglo-Saxon insistence on a *passive* organism, in which associations are formed by the interplay of processes (such as temporal contiguity), and the occurrence of rewards and punishments) assuring successful *adaptation* to the environment" (Gray, 1966, pp. 1–2).

C. Linguistics. The next point of distinction regards the understanding of Russian *linguistics*. Long ago Weinreich made the observation that Russian linguistics has never been preoccupied with semantics; as well, there has never been a feeling in Russia that semantics would solve many of the linguistic problems it faced, according to Weinreich. This approach differed from the Bloomfieldian position, which rejected a mentalist approach to semantics, favoring the scientific method of observation. Russian linguistics has produced world-renowned scholars,[12] and during the 1920s it was influenced by poetry, the theater (Stanislavsky,[13] in particular), semiotics, and a special concept of semiotics of the filmmaker and friend of Vygotsky, Sergei Eisenstein. Topics ranging from Russian Formalism and linguistic structuralism to phonology represented an intrinsic part of Russian linguistics in the 1920s, and all students studying at Moscow University during that period were required to take courses in linguistics.[14] In viewing the history of psychology in Russia, which affected the development of linguistics, around the mid-1930s much of the progressive intellectual atmosphere was destroyed as a result of ideological battles. There was a return to the Pavlovian approach to psychology in 1950,[15] using the "second signal stimulus" (i.e., human speech)[16]

---

[12]"It is known that as early as pre-World War I an outstanding linguistic school was established in Russian science, represented by such scholars as Baudouin de Courtenay (1845–1929), F. F. Fortunatov (1848–1914), E. D. Polivanov (1890–1937), L. V. Ščerba (1880–1944), G. O Vinokur (1896–1947), and others. This Russian linguistic school—compromising in fact several directions, among them particularly the Moscow, Kazan, and Petersburg schools, which, however, all had certain common features—had of course its continuations in the twenties' and even later. Apart from historical comparative linguistics, it focused its interest on phonology and grammar on the one hand, and on the theory of poetic language and style and problems of social linguistics on the other. In the works of Baudouin de Courtenay, Fortunatov, Ščscherba, and other linguists, who undertook to discover new theoretical conceptions based on the framework of the then prevailing neogrammatical linguistics, we find one of the roots of later linguistic structuralism. This very background then gave rise to a generation of structuralists such as R. O. Jakobson, N. S. Trubetzkoy, S. I. Karcevskij, V. V. Vinogradov, and others, some of whom became co-authors of the linguistic theory of the Prague school in the twenties' and thirties' " (Průcha, 1972, pp. 29–30).

[13]For a good introduction to the acting principles of K. S. Stanislavsky, refer to N. B. Berkhin (1988, p. 3).

[14]"It should be pointed out that at the University of Moscow linguistics was one of the few subjects of instruction that were obligatory for all the students at the faculty. Here too was found the influence of one of the most important schools of linguistics of the period, the Moscow School, and its head, Filip Fedorovich Fortunatov (1848–1914)" (Jakobson & Pomorska, 1983, p. 10).

[15]During June/July of 1950 the Pavlov Conference took place, establishing the "Pavlovization" of psychology. The results of this conference had long-term effects on Russian psychology. For more information see T. R. Payne (1968, p. 94). It is interesting to read documentation on how scholars dealt with the new approach. Vocate (1987, p. 155) describes how Luria dealt with it, stating "To unite the basic reductionism of Pavlov with the moderate materialism of Marxism-Leninism is an almost impossible task since the two are essentially incompatible world views (Payne, 1968). Luria solved the problem by assimilating what he considered to be Pavlov's legitimate tenets on the physiological level, and using them in pursuing the origins of voluntary behavior via the combined motor

to describe language. This trend forced Russian psychology into a neo-Pavlovian concept of theory building and research, which in many respects returned to experiments examining higher order nervous system activity, otherwise known as the lower mental processes. The philosophical context Vygotsky brought to psychology was banned until 1956, although interest in Vygotsky persisted quietly during those years. During the 1960s there was great interest in Russia in the generative model of American linguistics; however, some of the major differences revolved around the fact that linguistic research in Russia was not reduced to "the construction of abstract models of the structure of language" (Průcha, 1972, p. 36). From this perspective, A. A. Leontiev in 1967 gave a list of criticisms of Chomsky's linguistic theory, which included:

> (1) In transformational psycholinguistics linguistic competence and performance models are constantly mixed; models produced by linguists and a linguistic way of thinking, directed towards the description of units and their properties and not towards the process involved, are transferred into psycholinguistics. (2) The greatest shortcoming of the Chomsky–Miller model is that motivation and any "pre-grammar" stage in speech encoding are completely ignored. (3) The classic experiment of Miller (1962b) and further experimental verifications of the generative model prove only the possibility of transforming sentences, but not the actual way of generating them. (4) The generative model is a theory of an exclusively unconscious use of language and does not include a description of various forms of conscious processes in speech activity. (5) The conclusions of the experimental verifications of the generative model cannot be generalized since they relate to the form of speech alone (monological, written form, isolated sentences with no context), whereas the psychological conditionality of the production of other forms of speech (especially the spoken form) is apparently very different. (quoted in Průcha, 1972, p. 81)

D. Psycholinguistics. In the United States the teaching of foreign languages is primarily subsumed under the theoretical construct of second language acquisition and applied linguistics; however, in Russia it is normally placed within *psycholinguistics.* What is often misunderstood by critics of Vygotsky and of *Activity Theory* is the fact that Russian and American psycholinguistics maintain a different genetic (e.g., beginning)– developmental historical line of research, and this has resulted in general misunderstandings from the very beginning, such as:

---

method . . . Pavlovian theory was adequate in Luria's opinion to explain lower mental functions, and the combined motor method resembled Pavlovian conditioning experiments. This solution was particularly ingenious, according to Cole (1979), because of its focus on speech. . . ." . . . In order to view the trend of Pavlovization during the 1950s, the book *Psychology in the Soviet Union*, edited by Brian Simon (1957), offers articles written by many of the well-known Russian psychologists writing for the most part within a Pavlovian framework.

[16]"Second signal system is a specific human system of cognitioned responses to verbal stimuli (no appearance with animals)" (Průcha, 1972, p. 13).

American psycholinguistics was born early in the fifties. Its foundations were in behavioristic psychology and thus it was almost synonymous with behavioristic learning theory. This mechanistic outlook . . . was unable to explain the richness of rational, conscious, integrative facts and context related to language and communication. Unfortunately, the assimilation of psycholinguistics into behaviorism generated its initial attack by non-behaviorists. Early adoption of psycholinguistic trends into applied linguistics was usually confined to the audio-lingual method of foreign language teaching, which involved repetition of pattern drills and memorizing dialogues which lead to a mechanical acquisition that was fraught with problems. (Slama-Cazacu, 1983, p. 267)

It is important to know that the terms *applied linguistics* and *sociolinguistics* have different meanings in Russia than in the West. Second language acquisition (SLA), for example, could be placed under the term *psycholinguistics or applied linguistics* in Russia, and SLA would maintain an initial *sociolinguistic* understanding there, since the individual is understood to be a socialized being first, later growing into individualization. During the 1950s and 1960s *applied linguistics* in Russia was closely connected to mathematical linguistics, machine translation, artificial languages, teaching foreign languages, teaching the hearing and speech impaired, etc.[17] Without appropriate background knowledge of Russian psycholinguistics, it is easy to understand why there are initial misgivings about Vygotskian theory within mainstream American or European SLA.

E. Functionalism. The understanding of *functionalism* within a Russian context is important to grasp from the Western perspective. For example:

The following conception of language is quite common in Soviet functional linguistics: Language (in the sense of national language) is a socially and historically determined system of signs. Such language exists exclusively as a set of "sub-languages" ("pod"-jazyk), i.e., as a standard (literary) language with its various forms, dialects, slang, etc. The study of the nature of language and its "sub-languages" requires a socio-functional approach, i.e., explanation of concrete manifestations of linguistic performance taking place within various social groups and social formations, and pursuing various functions. (Průcha, 1972, pp. 40–41)

A footnote from Průcha (1972) stated that ". . . the concept of function (*funkcija*) is interpreted in terms of the 'role', 'purpose', or 'goal', of verbal means and messages in the process of the use of language" (p. 40). A revised definition of *functionalism* is pivotal to a basic understanding of Russian thought, and it can be explained within the framework of A. R. Luria (who collaborated with Vygotsky):

. . . Luria has developed the concept of a "functional system" from a neuropsychological point of view. He has emphasized that, in such global functional systems as memory, there are many links in a cognitive process, some of which may be damaged in certain types of brain lesions. In some cases the functional system can be reinstated

[17]See Průcha (1972, p. 35).

if the disrupted link in the chain can be replaced with another link that is functionally equivalent. The idea of a functional system has been instrumental in Luria's constant struggle against strict localization theories of brain function . . . and global theories . . . (Wertsch, 1981, p. 20)

Russian functionalism is sometimes a difficult concept to understand in the West because it can refer to positions of abstract process patterns, which then oppose the physical realizations of those patterns leading into models of encoded symbols (e.g., Piaget). The word *functionalism* can refer to information-processing approaches, often used in Western psychology as a type of empiricism, constructing low-level models that account for data in particular studies (cf. Bickhard and Richie, 1983, p. 93). Within the psychology of language, Michael Silverstein refers to referential function and to pragmatic function 1 and 2, with other examples, many of which assume different philosophical positions. These are just a few of the interpretations of *functionalism*, and perhaps one of the major elements of *functionalism* is simply omitted, which includes the element of "time," whereas structuralism focuses on "space." Many misunderstandings have arisen regarding both functionalism and structuralism, which by necessity must operate together in a contextualized setting within both *time* and *space*. The Russian understanding of *functionalism* is different from the Western definition and should not be conflated with other theories, such as *systems approach*, *inter alia*.

F. Structure–Structuralism.   The next problem area relates to the concept *structure of activity* that has nothing to do with the current Western understanding of *structuralism*:

. . when Soviet psychologists speak of the *structure of an activity*, they have in mind something very different from what has come to be known as "structuralism" in Western psychology. The units they use are defined on the basis of the function they fulfill rather than of any intrinsic properties they possess. (Wertsch, 1981, p. 19)

The structuralism of Saussure and later of Chomsky take an idealized approach and should not be compared with the Russian understanding of the same term.

G. Aspect of Development.   The Western understanding of the word *developmental* usually means child development, or developmental psychology. The *genetic–developmental approach* lies at the heart of the Vygotskian approach and implies a beginning point of analysis (hence, *genetic*), viewing the *process* of development along various lines:

[A]

Calling his psychology "developmental" (geneticheskii—from genesis), Vygotsky meant much more than a mere analysis of the unfolding of behavior in ontogenesis. As a matter of fact, the very idea of development as unfolding and as maturation was alien to him. Vygotsky perceived psychological development as a dynamic process full of upheavals, sudden changes, and reversals. This process, however, ultimately leads to the formation of the cultural, higher mental functions. (Kozulin, 1986, p. 266)

[B]

One of the basic premises of this concept is that human development "is oriented towards establishing increasing autonomy of the person relative to its environment" (Valsiner, 1996, p. 120).

In Russian psychology the ongoing process of development offers an overall view of the individual within change. The Vygotskian approach takes child development from the perspective of *potential growth* of the child, emphasizing process over product. The beginning point of growth or the initial genetic aspect to be studied follows the progression of problem-solving activities within a method called "dual or double stimulation," which is discussed in detail. Within psychological experimentation Vygotsky would research the use of nonsense words and physical descriptions that would then allow the child time to progress within the *potential* for solving the problems under adult supervision. Although Vygotsky wrote about specific ages of periodization (e.g., stages) of development, his overall understanding was more *descriptive* than *prescriptive*, more focused on *process* rather than *product*. The underlying tenor of Vygotsky's understanding of development related to the emergence of personality, metaphorically comparing the actual age of the child with the potential age created under adult supervision within the zone of proximal development. There was a logical connection of the everyday world of the child being mediated and enhanced by the educational experience.

H. Establishing Adult Theories from Childs Psychology.   The question has often been raised concerning the extrapolation of Vygotsky's ideas regarding child development onto adult learning processes. This problem has not been solved and will not be solved in the future since there is no universal answer. One piece of the puzzle can be found in the difference between the concepts *incidental* and *intentional.* Alex Kozulin and Barbara Presseisen (1995) stated it this way: "The major contribution of the mediating adult is to turn the interactive situation from incidental to intentional" (p. 70). A simple definition of adult *intent* was given by Dore (Bruner, 1974–75), underscoring the fact that "communicative intent be defined as the inducement in a listener of the speaker's expectation" (p. 267). Of course, *intentionality* is not a characteristic of adults only, and in Vygotskian terminology, as children activate "object-regulation," moving on to "other-regulation," somewhere between the two areas there is *intentionality.* Up to that time, adults impute communicative intent to infants' utterances, where "many young children experience extensive verbal interchanges with their mothers. During these the mother actively picks up, interprets, comments upon, extends, repeats, and sometimes misinterprets what the child has said" (Ryan, 1974, p. 199). Jerome Bruner stated that communicative intent seems to be present from the start or very near the start. And intent of this kind uses whatever props are available. It is almost always in the interest of fulfilling his communicative intentions that the child recognizes and picks up new structural tricks relating to language. (Bruner, 1985, p. 27)

Regarding the adult, however,

The dual process of shaping and being shaped through culture implies that humans inhabit "intentional" (constituted) worlds within which the traditional dichotomies of subject and object, person and environment, and so on, cannot be analytically separated and temporally ordered into independent and dependent variables . . . Jerome Bruner's (1990) vision of cultural psychology also emphasizes the premise that human experience and action are shaped by our intentional states. It locates the emergence and function of psychological processes within the social-symbolically mediated everyday encounters of people in the lived events of their everyday lives. (Cole, 1996, p. 103)

In this context it should be stated that the philosophy of intentionality (e.g., phenomenology) is not included, and as Bruner has suggested, "if only for methodological reasons, I would propose that we avoid *a priori* arguments about 'conscious intent' and 'when' it is born" (Bruner, 1974/75, p. 266). In closing, the word *intention* is mentioned in many writings on *activity theory*,[18] and perhaps the most cogent statement given on this aspect is from Ivana Marková (1990) speaking of Bakhtin:

Words, he [Bakhtin] points out, do not live in some neutral and impersonal language but in other people's mouths and contexts, and as expressions of their intentions. Words are "appropriated" by the individuals who use them. . . . A word becomes "one's own" only when one populates it with one's own intention, own accent, adapting it to one's own semantic and expressive intention. (p. 135)

CONCLUSION

In pointing out some possible areas of misunderstanding between Western and Russian terminology it is hoped that readers will adopt a critical view of their

---

[18]Regarding the concept of "intention," Jean-Paul Bronckart (1995, p. 77) stated: "To answer the questions outlined in the preceding section, it is fitting to recall the distinction made by Elizabeth Anscombe (1957) in her volume *Intention*. She distinguished between 'events produced in nature' and 'human actions.' The statement 'Two tiles fell off the roof due to the effect of the wind' describes an *event* (the falling of the tiles), and this event may be explained. That is to say, one may attribute a cause, in the classical sense proposed by Hume (an antecedent logically independent of the event and capable of being identified separately). The statement 'I arranged for two tiles to fall off the roof to damage my neighbor's car' also describes an event that may be interpreted in a causal manner.

own interpretations of Vygotsky. Some of the basic theories in Western–Cartesian thought are often assumed to take on an isomorphic relationship within the Russian or European understanding of Vygotskian theory. The following area of possible confusion is emphasized for further thought and concludes this section: *Activity* and *action* remain the basic unit of analysis within a sociocultural and activity theory approach. However, from a cultural–historical perspective, remaining true to the origins of Vygotskian theory, there is an important focus on another aspect:

> *From action to thought.* Rather than a simple extension of a natural process originating in human biology, the higher mental process is a function of socially meaningful activity. This emphasis on the generative aspect of activity is theoretically significant, because it distinguishes Vygotsky's position from that of the "substantialists" who envisaged the material substance of the brain or the spiritual substance of Mind as the true seat of mental function. Vygotsky's position was the opposite: higher mental function is created through activity . . . The traditional rationalist formula, from thought to action, is thus reversed and becomes, from action to thought. (Kozulin, 1990, pp. 113–114)

It is hoped that readers in the Cartesian tradition will not attempt to *squeeze* a Vygotskian approach into the Western context, but will establish a dialogue with the Russian–Spinozian background in order to expand and clarify existing positions, all of which will help to retain the *dialectic* needed for Vygotskian theory to expand in a direction true to its origins.

Days and Ages

Lev Semonovich Vygotsky's life and works served a purpose beyond himself, one of understanding and co-creating a better world. It is with that view in mind that the following thoughts are dedicated. Vygotsky's life and legacy can be viewed within a continuum that spanned an exciting period of history, one in which utopian ideals were a living presence, a potential for real societal change.

In viewing the life of Vygotsky one must recreate parts of the puzzle for oneself since no autobiography has been located to date among the 180 to 200 works he wrote. Since many of his articles have not yet been published or translated into English, and because his interests were so broad, many scholars tend to analyze parts of his overall framework that do not always offer a complete picture. As well, his works were banned in Russia until 1956. In beginning a short summary of Vygotsky's life, Newman & Holzman (1993) presented a composite picture of the vastness of Vygotsky's general interests, stating that:

> But since it also describes a human action, it should moreover be analyzed as referring to an *action*, involving an agent (e.g., human organism endowed with the ability to act, or a capacity for action), a *motive* (or reason for acting), and thus a *purpose* (a plan)."

Here is a man who, while an adolescent, staged Gogel's *The Marriage*, published a literary critique, wrote an essay on Hamlet which became the basis for his dissertation, led a Jewish study circle . . . who could read and speak eight languages . . . who during his twenties founded several literary magazines, authored a theater column, lectured on history, literature, theater and science, read widely in philosophy, linguistics, history and psychology, who, after becoming a renowned psychologist in Moscow, returned to medical school as a first-year student, co-directed an art seminar, consulted frequently with film director Eisenstein, held numerous political and scientific posts, and conducted practical education intervention with handicapped and retarded children. (p. 157)

Lev Semonovich was greatly influenced by German philosophers and psychologists[19] and became interested in Hegelian dialectics around the age of 15, using this concept the rest of his life as an analogy for change within the dynamic process of development. His interest in Marx as a classical philosopher was intense. In fact, Vygotsky attempted to write *Mind in Society* as a *Kapital* for psychology using the concept of *word meaning* as a psychological unit of analysis of consciousness, just as Marx applied the term *cell* relating to society. Vygotsky was also influenced by the writings of Spinoza, whose thoughts on one *substance* (which was either nature or God) and *attributes* (extensions of the substance) gave a sense of the immutable and provided a framework of stability for Vygotsky. At the same time, the basic understanding of Spinozian *substance* and *monism* were understood as being dynamic principles anchored within a changing higher level of understanding, all of which transcended traditional Cartesian dualisms.

While still a young man Vygotsky became very interested in the arts and the aesthetics, all of which were later used for the development of his psychological theories on consciousness and culture. Vygotsky's approach was invariably *metatheoretical* and *metapsychological* (Moll, 1992), as well as being *metapragmatic* and *metasematic* (Wertsch, 1985b). Understanding Vygotsky as a metatheoretican is of utmost importance in comprehending the intentions of his writings. Vygotsky was an outsider to psychology, which created criticism regarding various aspects of his points of view, such as his understanding of the terms *consciousness, word meanings as a unit of analysis,* and other constructs that were ultimately approached from a philosophical stance.[20]

[19]"Vygotsky's sources were, mainly, German, Russian, and North American. Authors frequently quoted were Wundt, Brentano, Stumpf, Ebbinghaus, Ach, Bühler, Meinong, Lipps, Stern, Husserl, Binswanger, Dilthey, Münsterberg, Freud, Adler, Uexküll, Wertheimer, Köhler, and Koffka, among the Germans; Chelpanov, Bekhterev, Pavlov, Kornilov, Blonski, and Vagner, among the Russians; and James, Dewey, Baldwin, Thorndike, and Watson, among the North Americans. Together with these authors, psychologists of diverse nationalities are also quoted, such as Titchener, Claparède, Janet, and Piaget. There are also references to physicists of the time such as Einstein and Planck" (Rosa & Montero, 1992, p. 76).

[20]Referring to Vygotsky: "He remained, however, an outsider with respect to psychology, no matter how paradoxical it sounds nowadays, when he is widely regarded as the father of Soviet

Vygotsky was a "top-down" philosopher, meaning that he took the highest level of explanation possible, usually the highest aesthetic element available, and proceeded along a genetic–developmental continuum in order to discover the paths that led to the corresponding development.[21] "Top-down" should not be equated with elitism but rather with the attempt to measure oneself by the highest explanatory principle. Vygotsky felt that culture must be handed down to future generations, since culture is not biologically inherited and could be lost.

During his life Vygotsky suffered in many ways, fighting bouts of tuberculosis, even thinking he would die in his twenties. Vygotsky's strength of character was born out of simple gestures that are often overlooked today; for example, the fact that Vygotsky openly quoted the controversial Russian poet Osip Mandelstam was an act of courage itself during the 1930s.[22]

Vygotsky died on June 11, 1934, leaving behind a legacy that remains contemporary today. The disciplines Vygotsky has influenced worldwide are tremendous, and just a few are listed:

> Areas of research influenced by Vygotsky include play (Elkonin [El'konin], 1980), the evolution of children's drawing (e.g., Vygotsky, 1982a), literate codes (Azcoaga, 1982), and the nature of thought disturbance in certain schizophrenics (Goldstein, 1958). Ivanov (1971) considers Vygotsky's work a precursor to cybernetics, the science of control, communication, and information, and semiotics. Vygotsky also developed new disciplines: neuropsychology (Blanck, 1989a), neurolinguistics (Luria, 1980), psycholinguistics (Azcoaga, 1984b), and the psychology of art (Blanck, 1989b; Vygotsky, 1971). His theories have had implications in the fields of aesthetics (Morawski, 1977), literary criticism (Ambrogio, 1975), the psychology of creativity (Vygotsky, 1936, 1982a), defectology (Meshchernyakov, 1985), transcultural psychology

psychology. His approach was essentially "methodological," focused on the elaboration of what is or ought to be the *subject* of psychological inquiry, and which *method* of study psychology should take on to fit its objectives; but such a task belongs not so much to professional psychology as to philosophy" (Kozulin, 1994, p. xxxix).

[21]Vygotsky's position as a *top-down* methodologist was reflected in many of these lines of thought, especially in education. He firmly believed that culture should be passed down to future generations, certainly in a Socratic, not dogmatic way. This *top-down* approach should not be viewed as elitist, since Vygotsky believed that everyone should be given the tools to live up to his or her highest potential, which he demonstrated by traveling around Russia to work on various projects; as well, his work with the mentally challenged is a basic part of his entire research, and one should not forget his strong desire to help establish a new society which would reflect Marxist principles. The following is a quote regarding Vygotsky's *top-down* approach to art, specifically to the analysis of the fable: "Both Potebnia and Lessing proceeded from the bottom up, from the fable to the higher forms of literature. We shall operate in the reverse manner and begin our analysis at the top, applying to the fable all the psychological rules governing the higher forms of poetry" (Vygotsky, 1971 [1925], p. 93).

[22]"It is probably difficult for a non-Soviet reader to understand what it meant for a scientist in 1934 to quote Mandelstam, who by that time was repressed, or Gumilyov, already shot by a firing squad. This was not just an act of civic courage; we believe this shows that Vygotsky understood that the days of the culture to which he himself belonged were numbered" (Sobkin & Leontiev, 1992, p. 186).

(Scribner & Cole, 1981), cognitive anthropology (Goody, 1977), and education (Bruner, 1971), not excluding his important metatheoretic contributions (Puzirei, 1986; Rivière, 1985). (Blanck, 1992, p. 49)

There are many views regarding the personality of Vygotsky, but a very personal side of Vygotsky has been revealed by his oldest daughter, Gita L'vovna, in stating that

> Lev Semonovich was not at all asectic, uninterested in anything but his science, who would not notice anything around him. He was a very lively, emotional person who knew well the entire scale of human emotions. He, like nobody else, could empathize and share a person's sorrow, but he was also very happy and lively with friends. He had a wonderful sense of humor, loved and appreciated a joke, could make jokes himself. And yet, at the same time, he was always a very modest, extremely delicate human being. (Vygodskaia, 1995, p. 59)

V. V. Davydov and V. P. Zinchenko have also stated the following:

> Now let us say a few words about Vygotsky as a person. According to our teachers, he was a good person, passionate and exacting of both himself and others. Knowledge, feeling and will were harmoniously intermingled in him, which made him a true scholar, one whose life and works served as a model for many generations of Soviet psychologists. (Davydov & Zinchenko, 1993, p. 105)

Another description of Vygotsky the person is:

> One of the translators (J. K.) had the good fortune to meet [Vygotsky]. He was a man of great vision, almost clairvoyant in understanding the schizophrenic; . . . Vigotsky [Vygotsky] was a man of unusual personal charm, kind, extremely idealistic, and passionately zealous in teaching, the source of his greatest satisfaction. Needless to say he was an outstanding linguist. (S. Saporta, 1961, p. 537)

In fact the only negative comment to be heard or read about Vygotsky the person (in English translations) was given by one of his followers, Piotr Gal'perin:

> When he saw a depicted or displayed representation of something he didn't understand anything about it, he could say what he saw, but he had no grasp of the reference, the meaning or the quality of it. On the other hand, if he had to tell somebody else about this very representation, he came up with more than that person could see in it. With him, everything emerged in speech! . . . According to Gal'perin (1986a), this aspect of Vygotsky's personality bordered on pathology, because it was not explainable as merely one-sidedness. You speak of one-sidedness, when one personality trait is more strongly developed than another. With Vygotsky, however, it was more a question of the complete absence of something. In Gal'perin's view, it was something like agnosia, but that wasn't really it either. Vygotsky knew, for example, that a particular object was a chair. But that chair held no meaning for him; if put into words, then he could tell you everything about that chair: the history of it, the part it played in the life of the man who sat on it, etc . . . Apart from this, Gal'perin (1986a) remembered Vygotsky as a socially extrovert person, active, but detached in human relationships. He always stayed at some distance from people and that applied not only to outsiders

... Anyway, Vygotsky was an exceptional, verbally gifted person, who made a great impression on Gal'perin as well. (quoted in J. Haenen, 1996, pp. 28–29)

Gal'perin was of the opinion "that Vygotsky was the only real man of genius in the history of Russian and Soviet psychology" (Haenen, 1996, p. 27); and yet Gal'perin "disagreed with Vygotsky's theoretical assumptions on the basis of his own research, and went his own way. Apparently, Alexksei Nikolaevich Leont'ev [Leontiev] was more instrumental to Gal'perin's development as a psychologist than Vygotsky" (Haenen, 1996, p. 29).

In closing, the daughter of Vygotsky, Gita L'vovna, has given a short summary of her feelings regarding her father:

My father always talked to us peacefully, kindly . . . We loved each other very much. Perhaps it is not even necessary to say how I cherished our relationship. We were connected by real friendship . . . When kids would drop by, we would start playing right there beside him, while he would sit at his desk, working and from time to time turning around and looking with a smile as we played before immersing himself in his work again. One has to wonder how he managed, under such conditions, to achieve so much . . . In addition to ourselves, Lev Semenovich's parents (my grandfather and grandmother), four of his unmarried sisters, and his older sister with her husband and son, lived in our apartment. The family in which I spent my childhood was very big and friendly . . . Lev Semenovich worked very much, way too much. And when he died, his relatives did not have to ponder long what to bury him in: He had only one suit. To us, his children, he left the most important, dearest thing parents can leave to their children: good memories of him and a good, spotlessly clean name. (Vygodskaia, 1995, pp. 57–59)

2

Overview of L. S. Vygotsky's
Psychological–Philosophical Theory

The approach Vygotsky took was instrumental (until 1930), cultural, and historical,[23] where

> "Instrumental" referred to the basically mediated nature of all complex psychological functions. Unlike basic reflexes, which can be characterized by a stimulus–response process, higher functions incorporate auxiliary stimuli, which are typically produced by the person himself . . . The "cultural" aspect of Vygotsky's theory involved the socially structured ways in which society organizes the kinds of tasks that the growing child faces and the kinds of tools, both mental and physical, that the young child is provided to master those tasks . . . The "historical" element merged into the cultural one. (Luria, 1979, p. 44)

Many of Vygotsky's theories were derived from other thinkers of the times, viewed through a filter of *critical assimilation* (Moll, 1992, p. 52). The results led to an entirely new philosophical foundation in Russian psychology, with a focus on understanding the higher mental and cultural processes, together with the lower stimulus–response approach. A more complete understanding of the higher mental processes was necessary for comprehending individual and societal growth, in particular within the area of education.

> "It is important to distinguish Vygotsky the *methodologist* from Vygotsky the *psychologist*,[24] emphasizing that the Russian understanding of methodology expands

---

[23]"Luria (1979) recalled that Vygotsky referred to his psychology as instrumental, cultural, and historical" (Blanck, 1992, p. 45).

[24]Some scholars have suggested other titles for Vygotsky rather than psychologist. "Wertsch . . . cautions against categorizing Vygotsky as a psychologist, at least in the present meaning of the term. He characterizes him as a social theoretician" (Blanck, 1992, p. 40).

beyond the constraints of experimental research and empirical data collecting. Within the Russian understanding of methodology there is a philosophical approach of establishing a higher order of theory. Perhaps two of the best labels given to Vygotsky have been *cultural theorist* (Wertsch, 1985b), and *interpretivist* (Bruner in Rieber, 1987).

CONSCIOUSNESS

From a Western perspective the study of *consciousness* presents a somewhat odd and strange approach to understanding Russian psychology, linguistics, and psycholinguistics. In the Russian tradition, *consciousness*[25] begins within a socialized context where adults and outside situations first help to mediate understanding for children, and where that experience and knowledge are then internalized or appropriated. In other words, adults gesture, mimic, and afford contextualized meaning to the child, and later the child internalizes or appropriates meaning for him/herself via a long continuum of *concept developments*. Perhaps the most quoted statement of Vygotsky has been the *general genetic law of cultural development*, which states that "any function in the child's cultural development appears twice or on two planes . . . It appears first between people as an intermental category, and then within the child as an intramental category" (Vygotsky, 1987, p. 21).

One aspect of the core of Vygotsky's understanding of psychology from 1925 until his death in 1934 was *consciousness* used as the highest explanatory principle. Vygotsky defined *consciousness* in his notes as: "(1) knowledge in connection; (2) consciousness (social) . . . Semiotic analysis is the only adequate method for the study of the systemic and semantic structure of consciousness" (taken from Vygotsky's notes found in A. N. Leont'ev's [Leontiev] private archives in Rieber & Wollock, 1997, p. 137).

The problem of the definition of *consciousness* has presented difficulty within the history of psychology because any scholar as an individual is placed in the situation of not knowing many of the ontological answers to the universe. The entire concept of *consciousness* has been so unsettling that many scholars in areas such as *behaviorism* have tried to do away with it altogether.

---

[25]For a good explanation of the Russian understanding of *consciousness* see V. V. Davydov & L. A. Radzikhovskii (1985, pp. 38–49). For example, "Vygotsky (1925) considered consciousness, first, as a 'reflex of reflexes' (it being clarified that he had in mind something like a reflex arc with reverse connections (p. 198), second, as the 'problem of the structure of behavior' (p. 181), and third, as an issue in human labor activity (p. 197)." (p. 38). The article being referred to in this quote is from Vygotsky, "Consciousness as a problem in the psychology of behavior." In *Soviet Psychology* (1979a, Vol. 27(4), pp. 3–35). Also refer to Leontiev (1978 and 1981).

With the advent of behaviorism in 1913 the mind–body problem disappeared—not because ostrich-like its devotees hid their heads in the sand but because they would take no account of phenomena which they could not observe. The behaviorist finds no mind in his laboratory—sees it nowhere in his subjects . . . If the behaviorists are right in their contention that there is no observable mind–body problem and no observable separate entity called mind—then there can be no such thing as consciousness and its subdivisions. (J. Watson, 1966 [1928], pp. 93–94)

Implementing an objective, scientific method of observation was the wish of many American psychologists at the turn of the 20th century, wanting to go beyond philosophical debates generated at universities such as Leipzig, Germany. Indeed, when Bloomfield returned from his studies in Germany he simply wanted to establish a method of objective observation as opposed to the introspectionist philosophy of mentalism. His view was understandable when one looks up a definition of *consciousness* in a dictionary. For example:

Consciousness . . . A designation applied to conscious mind as opposed to a supposedly unconscious or subconsciousness mind and to the whole domain of the physical and nonmaterial. Consciousness is generally considered an indefinable term or rather a term definable only by direct introspective appeal to conscious experiences. The indefinability of consciousness is expressed by Sir William Hamilton: "Consciousness cannot be defined: we may be ourselves fully aware what consciousness is, but we cannot without confusion convey to others a definition of what we ourselves clearly apprehend. The reason is plain: consciousness lies at the root of all knowledge."[26]

Since much of Russian intellectual life was based in part on the philosophical tradition of Germany, discussions on *consciousness* did not simply disappear after the Russian revolution, even with the advent of the Pavlovian approach. These discussions were anchored in conceptual areas such as *action, language, social, and so on*. However, during the 1950s the study of *consciousness* took on a different understanding in Russia:

The Soviet doctrine of consciousness is tied to action not only in that consciousness is accorded an important role in directing man's actions, but also in that it is shaped by the results of his actions. . . . According to the Leninist theory of reflection consciousness is developed in man's purposive action on the world which exists externally of him. Thus, consciousness does not evolve from the "immanent laws" of its internal dynamics (Hegel's position), but it develops in interaction with the "real" world. . . . Therefore, it is argued, one must study man in action to understand his consciousness. (Bauer, 1959, p. 135)

It is important to remember that the *social* precedes the *individual* in Vygotsky's understanding of consciousness, and that it is created and expanded through interaction with the world, and "like Marx, Vygotsky . . . argued that 'the social dimension of consciousness is primary in time and fact. The individual

---

[26]Definition of Consciousness taken from Runes (Ed.), *Dictionary of philosophy*. New York: Philosophical Library. Quoted in Edinger (1984, p. 64).

dimension of consciousness is derivative and secondary, based on the social'"
(Wertsch, 1983, p. 22). Vygotsky stated that "this also means that consciousness
cannot focus on itself, that it is a secondary and derivative activity" (Vygotsky,
1979a, p. 27). A basic part of Vygotsky's ethics is derived from the assumption
that how we react to others is how we view ourselves; or

> the mechanism of social behavior and the mechanism of consciousness are the same
> ... We are aware of ourselves, for we are aware of the other, and in the same way as
> we know others; and this is as it is because we in relation to ourselves are in the same
> (position) as others are to us. ... (Kozulin, 1986, p. 265)

M. K. Mamardashvili (1990) stated a similar thought by saying that
"consciousness is primarily consciousness of the other" (p. 7). Basically,
consciousness is a response apparatus and once consciousness emerges it starts
to define life (cf. Kozulin, 1990, p. 245). This idea *inter alia* was taken from
Pierre Janet, who wrote that a person's personality is not innate, but is developed. "His [Janet's] main idea is that personality develops as we attribute to ourselves exactly the same features and attitudes that we first attributed to the
personality of others and that others attributed to us" (van der Veer & Valsiner,
1988, p. 57).[27]

The schema Vygotsky used for activating this understanding was as
follows: *collective (social) activity—culture—signs—individual activity—
individual consciousness.*[28] It is important to keep the understanding of *consciousness as an explanatory principle* separate from the means of assessing
partial results of the observation of *consciousness* by using *units of analysis.*
The first aspect can only be viewed metaphorically, since no one can step outside
of *consciousness* to observe it in its entirety:

> Thus, Vygotsky's first principle as a methdologist was as follows: It is necessary to
> identify the explanatory principle that defines the boundaries and structure of a theory
> ... However, this picture is incomplete as long as we do not address the question of
> the origin of the explanatory principle. This is a concept (as a rule semifunctional) that
> reflects a certain reality that, in turn, determines mental phenomena and makes
> possible their reconstruction. Vygotsky believed that explanatory principles that are
> relevant for psychology are philosophical conceptions that have been further devel-
> oped. They are borrowed from philosophy by psychologists ... Thus, according to
> Vygotsky, methodological analysis in psychology involves a twofold process: First, it
> begins with an existing theoretical apparatus ... Then it develops an explanatory prin-
> ciple and defines its place in a philosophical tradition. Then, conversely, Vygotsky
> envisioned the verification from the perspective of the logic of this philosophical
> tradition, a vertification of the application of the philosophical concept as an expla-
> natory principle in psychological theory and its development on the basic of the
> given explanatory principle. Vygotsky (1982, p. 55) himself called this the"logical–

[27]For a more detailed description of Pierre Janet, see his book L'évolution psychologique de la
personnalité (1929). Paris: A. Chahine.
[28]For a more detailed description see V. D. Davydov & V. P. Zinchenko (1989).

historical" method, in contrast to the "formal–logical–semantic" method. (Davydov and Radzikhovskii, 1985, pp. 50–51)

Although Vygotsky at one point called *consciousness* the *reflex of reflexes*,[29] he transcended this understanding by using the phrase *experience of experiences*,[30] later defining *consciousness* as *co-knowledge*.[31] "Rather than study reflexes, we must study behavior, its mechanisms, its component parts, and its structure" (Vygotsky, 1979a, p. 10). *Consciousness* is not an *a priori* that is given and it is not generative by nature, but originates in society. Therefore, "what is most remarkable in all this is that consciousness of speech and social experience occur simultaneously and completely in parallel with one another" (Vygotsky, 1979a, p. 31). It is at this point that speech and meaning start to evolve in the theory of *consciousness*, entering the realm of semiotics. In *The Problem of Consciousness* (Rieber and Wollock, 1997), Vygotsky began his notes on speech, stating that:

> Speech is a correlate of consciousness, not of thinking . . . Speech is a sign for the communication between consciousness . . . Consciousness as a whole has a semantic structure . . . Consciousness is prone to splintering. Consciousness is prone to merging. (they are essential for consciousness). . . . (pp. 136–137)

Returning to the connection of speech being correlated with meaning, David Bakhurst (1986) made the important statement that ". . . Vygotsky held the opinion that the focal point, the unit, of the new theory of consciousness was *meaning*" (p. 122), which will later be explored within functional interrelationships. Vygotsky distinguished between *consciousness* and *conscious awareness*, and it is only when "true concepts" are achieved that *conscious awareness* is fully understood. Therefore, both *intentionality* and *conscious awareness* are two fundamental concepts serving to bridge Vygotskian theory from child development to adult theory.[32]

Vygotsky was interested in closing the "mind/body" gap of Descartes, and in approaching a solution to this problem Bauer offered an understanding close to the Vygotskian perspective:

> The doctrine that "consciousness must be understood in action" combines with the dialectical principle of the "unity of form and content" (actually they are only aspects

---

[29]"Already in an article published in 1925 . . . we can see him [Vygotsky] formulating the idea that human consciousness has a social origin. At that time, however, Vygotsky still strongly thought along reflexological lines. He thought of consciousness as evolving through the incorporation of social reflexes. Our own reflexes (and especially words) can function as stimuli for new reflexes and consciousness is only the reflex of reflexes. In later years he discarded this idea" (van der Veer & Valsiner, 1988, p. 63).

[30]See van der Veer & Valsiner (1994, p. 33). Also see Vygotsky (1979a, p. 19).

[31]Related in A. N. Leontiev's "The problem of activity in psychology." *Soviet Psychology* (1972, Vol. 9, p. 19).

[32]cf. Roter (1987, p. 109).

of each other) to support a more concrete, and hence a more applied approach to the study of psychological processes. (Bauer, 1959, p. 136)[33]

Within the metatheoretical, metaphorical perspective presented by Vygotsky, the Spinozian philosophical understanding of monism, on a higher cosmic level, parallels *consciousness* as the highest explanatory principle on the individual level. "Monism was one of the central assumptions of the truly scientific and therefore Marxist methodology: mind and body constitute a single reality in the functioning human being, and therefore a single science must ultimately describe and explain the unity" (Joravsky, 1987, pp. 201–202).

Since Vygotsky took *consciousness* as the highest explanatory principle, he needed to find an instrument of analysis separate from *consciousness*;[34] this is where Vygotsky selected the concept of activity that maintained a different meaning from that given to it by the *Kharkov School of Activity Theory*, carried on by his students and followers after his death. With the aspects of *consciousness* and *culture* (including mediation) representing the basic elements of the highest level of Vygotsky's framework, it was established that "the key to the evolution of human consciousness and society lies in the linguistic mediation of consciousness" (Lee, 1987, p. 104). In general (but not exclusively), there are three types of mediation: *consciousness* (or mental activity), *social cooperation* (sociality), and tools (technology) (cf. Ratner, 1991, pp. 14–15). Humans must have *signs* in order to function and communicate, and it is important to keep in mind that the individual does not "confront things as a solitary consciousness" (Ratner, 1991, pp. 14–15).[35]

LOWER MENTAL PROCESSES AND HIGHER MENTAL PROCESSES

The lower mental processes are elementary perception, involuntary memory, localized attention, and so on, whereas the higher mental processes are

[33]"The most important consideration in our context is that Vygotsky saw a real philosophical alternative that provided a basis for transcending dualisms of mind and body, intellect and affect, involuntary and voluntary acts, etc., underlying the control paradigm in psychology of motivation and emotions" (Aidman & Leontiev, 1991, p. 141).

[34]See A. Kozulin (1994, p. 59), where Vygotsky stated that "this method of 'explaining' a thing by the very thing that needs explaining is the basic flaw of all intellectualistic theories." Also, see Levitin (1982, pp. 88–89), referring to Vygotsky: "His main premise as methodologist was that in any theory, one must first isolate an explanatory principle that delineates the theory's limits and structure. This general principle is distinct from the object under study and provides the unit of psychological analysis. Thus, researchers must find not a static, one-dimensional theory, but the dynamic relationship between 'the explanatory principle' and the object under study."

[35]Referring to *signs*: "This means that they are not simply invented or passed down by adults, but rather arise from something that is originally not a sign operation and that becomes one only after a series of qualitative transformations, each of which conditions the next stage and is itself

logical memory, creative imagination, verbal thinking and regulation, and similar processes. In other words, the lower mental processes are natural and the higher mental processes are cultural, with both areas needing to be intact for a human being to function on a higher level. "If one decomposes a higher mental function into its constitutional parts, one finds nothing but the natural, lower skills . . . The latter assumption does not imply, however, that the higher functions can be reduced to lower ones" (Kozulin, 1986, p. 266). The concept of the lower–higher mental functions was originally taken from Thorndike in order to overcome the problem of dualism,[36] and in this respect Vygotsky talked about "the unity, but not the identity, of higher and lower psychological functions" (Vygotsky, 1994, p. 163). Vygotsky was not the originator of the distinction between the lower and higher mental processes, with both Oswald Külpe and Wilhelm Wundt having written about them years before.[37]

The importance of establishing the continuum of lower and higher mental processes (functions) revolves around changes, since

> the nature of development itself changes, from biological to socio-cultural. Verbal thought is not an innate, natural form of behavior but is determined by a historical-cultural process and has specific properties and laws that cannot be found in the natural forms of thought and speech. (Lee, 1987, p. 15)

Vygotsky distinguished between phases within the higher mental processes, beginning with the *rudimentary levels* and continuing with the advanced higher mental capacities. The connecting point between these two poles is *mediation*.

> Clearly Vygotsky viewed rudimentary and advanced higher mental functions in terms of a generic progression: the structure of [advanced] higher forms appears in a pure form in the psychological fossils, in these living remnants of ancient epochs. These rudimentary [higher] functions reveal to us the previous state of all [advanced] higher

conditioned by the preceding one an thus links them like stages of an integral process historical in nature" (van der Veer & Valsiner, 1991, p. 361).

[36]"Vygotsky's multidomain strategy avoids two fundamental forms of reductionism that often emerge in ontogenetic research. First, it avoids the pitfall of assuming that all aspects of cognitive development can be explained on the basis of principles devised to account for biological phenomena. With regard to contemporary theories, this is a point where Vygotsky's approach may be seen to differ from Piaget's. Rather than assuming that a single set of explanatory principles, such as adaptation and equilibration, can account for all aspects of cognitive development, Vygotsky argued that such principles need to be incorporated into a larger explanatory framework that deals with sociocultural phenomena as well. The second form or reductionism that Vygotsky was striving to avoid might be termed 'cultural reductionism,' because it rests on the premise that human psychological processes can be explained solely on the basis of mastery and internalization of symbolic means or sociocultural practices. Such accounts often ignore biological forces and other constraints involved in ontogenesis. Vygotsky clearly rejected what I am calling cultural reductionism, a fact reflected most clearly in his critique of idealism and subjective psychology" (Wertsch, 1985b, pp. 42–43).

[37]See R. van der Veer & M. H. van Ijzendoorn (1985, p. 1).

mental processes; they reveal the type of organization which they once possessed. (Wertsch, 1985b, p. 32)

There is a general assumption within Cartesian–Western thought that a single continuum does not exist between the lower and higher mental structures. Even within the Spinozist–Hegelian–Marxist tradition the understanding of a single continuum can only be perceived at the level of *monism* and not at the level of the dialectic. The element of connection is mediation and this can only be understood within Vygotsky's semiotics and the four domains Vygotsky analyzed.

DOMAINS: PHYLOGENY, ONTOGENY, SOCIOCULTURAL HISTORY, MICROGENESIS

Mediation is the means by which newer forms of higher order development occur. For example, the phylogenetic plane enters a higher level of development via collective labor and speech, whereas the ontogenetic plane enters the higher level via signs and mediated social interaction.[38] In understanding the developmental approach of lower and higher mental functions, Vygotsky maintained that higher mental functions should be used to analyze the lower mental processes. For example, Vygotsky used the philosophy of Spinoza and the understanding of *consciousness* as his highest explanatory principles, measuring everything in accordance with these ideas. There was, however, no attempt to attribute the development of higher level processes to one single explanatory principle.[39] There were four basic criteria that distinguished the lower from the higher mental processes:

[A]

(1) the shift of control from environment to the individual, that is, the emergence of voluntary regulation; (2) the emergence of conscious realization of mental processes; (3) the social origins and social nature of higher mental function; and (4) the use of signs to mediate higher mental functions. (Wertsch, 1985b, p. 25)

[B]

Unlike basic processes, higher functions are (1) self-regulated rather than bound to the immediate stimulus field; (2) social or cultural rather than biological in origin; (3) the object of conscious awareness rather than automatic and unconscious; and (4) mediated through the use of cultural tools and symbols . . . (Díaz, Neal, & Amaya-Williams, 1992, p. 128)

Historically it has been understood that Vygotsky's concept of lower and higher mental processes replaced Durkheim's *collective representations*, although

---

[38]Ibid., pp. 1–9.
[39]See Wertsch (1985b, p. 22).

these two areas cannot be totally positioned together, since Vygotsky felt that Durkheim[40] left out an adequate description of the genetic–developmental line and a sense of the dialectic. The problem now arises as to how Vygotsky traced the origins of the higher mental functions:

> "Higher mental functions" must have an origin; but this origin must not be sought in the depths of the spirit or hidden properties of nervous tissue: it must be sought outside the individual human organism in objective *social history*. . . . The formation of language during the process of social development provided him not only with a new, hitherto unknown method of communication but also with a new tool for ordering his mental processes. The higher mental functions which originated in social labor and speech enabled man to rise to a new plane of organization in his activity. (Luriya [Luria], 1967, p. 54)

At this point there needs to be an understanding between the areas of phylogeny (biological evolution) and ontogeny (human evolution), with both aspects incorporating the means of change for further development. On the phylogenetic level, Vygotsky focused on *process* and not so much on *product*, stating in *Mind in Society* that

> The concept of a historically based psychology is misunderstood by most researchers who study child development. For them, to study something historically means, by definition, to study some past event. Hence, they naively imagine an insurmountable barrier between historic study and study of present-day behavioral forms. *To study something historically means to study it in the process of change*; that is the dialectical method's basic demand . . . (Vygotsky quoted by Scribner in Tobach, 1997, p. 244)

In switching to the ontogenetic plane, the *social*[41] is appropriated via mediation and is *internalized* with a new understanding that is one of the most important ideas of Vygotsky. In ontogeny there is an interweaving of the *natural/biological*, *cultural*, and the *social*, all of which interact creating dynamic change.[42] "Further, Vygotsky makes the yet stronger claim that internalisation is the source of all the higher mental functions . . ." (Bakhurst, 1986, p. 116), with Vygotsky stating that "at first, other people act on the child. Then he/she emerges or enters into interaction with those around him/her. Finally, he/she begins to act on others, and only at the end begins to act on himself/herself" (Vygotsky, 1979b, p. 95). Since the *general genetic law of cultural development* is perhaps the most

---

[40]For more information on the comparisons and differences between Vygotsky and Durkheim, see van der Veer & Valsiner (1991, pp. 206–207).

[41]"Vygotsky stresses many times that we must not look for an explanation of higher mental processes in the brain since they were generated not by the brain, but by the process of social–historical development of humanity . . ." (Tulviste, 1991, p. 30).

[42]Wertsch (1991, p. 22)

quoted statement of Vygotsky, it will be repeated here in order to understand how *internalization*[43] is perceived by him:

> Any function in the child's cultural development appears twice, or on two planes. First it appears on the social plane, and then on the psychological plane. First it appears between people as an interpsychological category, and then within the child as an intrapsychological category. This is equally true with regard to voluntary attention, logical memory, the formation of concepts, and the development of volition . . . Social relations or relations among people genetically underlie all higher functions and their relationships. (Vygotsky in Wertsch, 1985b, pp. 60–61)

The concept of *history* for Vygotsky was not only equated with ontogenesis but with other domains as well, such as phylogenesis, which was divided into labor and speech.[44] Since Vygotsky did not feel that "biological laws can explain the emergence of higher forms of behavior in general, he rejected their explanatory value for these behaviors in child history as well" (Scribner, 1997, p. 246). Apart from human evolution (phylogenesis) and individual evolution (ontogenesis), another domain was *sociocultural* history. Within this area the concepts of tools–psychological tools–signs are discussed in depth in the next section. The last domain was *microgenesis*.[45] This aspect brings one to Vygotsky's methodology and research analysis, with Vygotsky being of the opinion that the higher mental processes could be evaluated objectively, not only introspectively.

> There were two types of microgenetic processes that interested him. First, he was concerned with the unfolding of a single psychological act (e.g., forming a precept); second, he was concerned with the developmental transitions that occur over the course of a training or experimental session. (Wertsch, 1990, p. 65)[46]

Davydov and Radzikhovskii have made the distinction between Vygotsky the *methodologist* and the *psychologist*,[47] and Vygotsky himself wrote that

---

[43]The term "internalization" is taken from *Hegel's* concept of *Verinnerlichung*. To avoid the problem and misunderstanding of simply transferring the external to the internal realm, James Wertsch uses the terms *appropriation* and *mastery* (Wertsch, 1998). It should, however, be stated that Vygotsky is clear on his concept of *internalization* by claiming that "During the process of 'interiorization,' i.e., the inward transfer of functions, there occurs a complex reconstruction of their entire structure . . . Entering into this new system, it [internalization] begins to function according to the laws of the whole of which it is now a part" (Vygotsky & Luria, 1994, p. 156).

[44]For an excellent description of history in most of the domains Vygotsky described, see Scribner (1997, pp. 241–265).

[45]For an article on the application of the microgenetic approach see Flavell & Draguns (1957).

[46]"As Wertsch & Stone (1978) have pointed out, the term *microgenesis* has been used in connection with two different phenomena. The first type of microgenesis refers to the gradual course of skill acquisition during an experimental or training session, and the second refers to the unfolding of percepts or concepts over a span of milliseconds" (Wertsch, 1981, p. 28).

[47]Wertsch (1985b, p. 43).

"The search for a method becomes one of the most important problems of the entire enterprise of understanding the uniquely human forms of psychological activity. In this case, the method is simultaneously prerequisite and product, the tool and the result of the study. In summary, then, the aim of psychological analysis and its essential factors are as follows: (1) process analysis as opposed to object analysis; (2) analysis that reveals real, causal or dynamic relations as opposed to enumeration of a process's outer features, that is, explanatory, not descriptive, analysis; and (3) developmental analysis that returns to the source and reconstructs all the points in the development of a given structure." (Vygotsky, 1978, p. 65)

In reviewing the psychological trends of his day, that is, introspectionism, zoopsychology, the reflexology of Bekhterev and Pavlov, and so on, Vygotsky discovered that they often did not incorporate the higher mental processes in their research.

Therefore, the higher levels of human behavior were extracted from the lower psychological process, leaving out immeasurable elements such as volition, will, motivation, and the like. In other words, psychology worked for the most part within the *stimulus–response* mode of experimentation. Another consideration was that of the *a priori* and *innatism.* Vygotsky attributed innatism to the lower mental processes, never trying to exclude this understanding in his theories. One could guess that if Vygotsky were alive today he would revise these thoughts substantially. He was of the strong opinion that "psychology must carve itself a path between *a priorism* and naked empiricism" (Vygotsky in Bakhurst, 1986, p. 107). Some of the concerns facing Vygotsky centered around a general misunderstanding that higher mental functions are extrapolated from *primitive* psychological mechanisms, which is not the case.[48] Another problem was the understanding that *mind* is located only in the head of an individual, that is, internally, leaving out the major premise of Vygotsky, namely that thinking processes are socialized first, then internalized. In order to establish a method that would take these problems into consideration, Vygotsky developed his account of the *instrumental act* between 1926 and 1930, using two approaches, with the first line of observation dealing with memory. Vygotsky used the works of Thurnwald, which in turn were taken from the Peruvian Quippu system of tying knots in order to remember things.[49] Vygotsky stated that "quite clearly, the line of direct memorizing is situated below that of indirect memorizing, and both show a certain tendency to grow according to the age of the child" (Vygotsky & Luria, 1994, p. 154). Any external device could be used in remembering or counting, such as fingers, straws, notches, and so on. The second approach revolved around experiments "to demonstrate how the child's behavior is restructured through the

[48]See Bakhurst (1986, p. 107).
[49]See van der Veer (1991, p. 86).

introduction of external sign-means and to explore how this behavior is internalized . . ." (Minick in Rieber, 1987, p. 22). The *instrumental act* was a unit of activity where tools or signs were used to monitor behavior:

> In 1930, then, Vygotsky abandoned the "instrumental act" and the "higher mental functions" as his unit and object of analysis, turning his attention to changes in interfunctional relationships, to the emergence and development of what he called "psychological systems." (Minick, 1987, p. 24)

Vygotsky turned his attention to the *word, word meaning, thought and language*, and *concept formation*, incorporating the functional aspect of thought and language, which was reflected in the development of the *method of double stimulation.*

> We regard the functional method of two-fold stimulation [usually referred to as the "functional *method of double stimulation*"—eds.] as most adequate to our task. Seeking to study the inner structure of the higher psychological processes, we do not limit ourselves to the usual method of offering the subject simple stimuli . . . to which we expect a direct response; we simultaneously offer a second series of stimuli which must play a functionally special role, serving as a means by which the subject can organize his own behaviour. In this way, we study the *process of accomplishing a task by the aid of certain auxiliary means*, and the whole psychological structure of the act thus proves to be within our reach over the entire course of its development and in all the variety of each of its phases. (Vygotsky & Luria, 1994, p. 159)

Although Vygotsky's research findings have been criticized,[50] his method containing the *experimental–developmental* approach remained true to his philosophical stance in general. For example, Vygotsky followed Lewin's concept of *phenotypes* (e.g., external features) and *genotypes* (e.g., internal features), where phenotypic meant *descriptive* and genotypic meant *explanatory.* "By a developmental study of a problem I [Vygotsky] mean the disclosure of its genesis, its causal dynamic basis. By phenotypic I mean the analysis that begins directly with an object's current features and manifestations" (Vygotsky, 1978, p. 62). Regarding an overview of Vygotsky's methods, one can perceive a transformation of his thoughts along a continuum from the instrumental act onward:

> The instrumental method in combination with a developmental approach suggested a full-scale program of research: a study of individual (ontogenetic) acquisition of psychological tools and the stages of transformation of natural psychological functions into "higher" ones; a study of the historical development of psychological tools and the corresponding development of higher mental functions; and finally a study of the most complex psychological tool, language, with respect to its formative role for human thought. (Kozulin, 1984, p. 106)

---

[50]For a review of criticisms given regarding the experimental results of Vygotsky's work, see van der Veer & Valsiner (1991, pp. 280–283).

Taken together, Vygotsky established four domains all relating to his concept of history: phylogenesis, ontogenesis, cultural–historical or sociocultural, and microgenesis. These areas are brought together under one heading of *sociogenesis*, claiming that all higher psychological functions (processes) have a social origin. Much of the credit given to this concept goes to Pierre Janet, who influenced Vygotsky tremendously in this respect. Janet also fought against a reductionist, behavioristic approach to human behavior, believing that behaviorism dealt with the lower mental processes only (cf. van der Veer & Valsiner, 1988, p. 56).

One of the areas Vygotsky did not write about was the specific nature of the influence of *institutions* on the developmental changes of all four domains. Michael Cole has since filled this gap by offering and expanding upon the concept *mesogenetic*:

> In the research to be described here, my colleagues and I have adopted what might be called a "mesogenetic" approach to cultural mediation, one whose time scale falls between the microgenetic scale employed in classical studies, where children are confronted with a difficult problem and their use of new mediational means is studied, and the macrogenetic scale implied by the historical difference between peasant and industrialized societies. The basic strategy for this research has been to create a system of activities with its own standing rules, artifacts, social roles, and ecological setting, that is, its own culture. (Cole, 1995b, p. 194)

Cole used this term to describe his *5th Dimension Project* that has taken on characteristics and a life of its own. The project is an extended computer game within sociocultural–historical ground rules, where children and parents work together to achieve graded levels of competency. Collaboration between various institutional settings and community organizations take place within this model. The *mesogenetic* aspect is important today, not only to monitor institutional–cultural influences, but to allow a faster rate of evaluation than is normally found within phlyogenetic and ontogenetic growth.

The next chapter deals specifically with the cultural–historical domain, viewing tools–psychological tools–signs, leading into a discussion of thought and language.

Tools–Psychological
Tools–Internalization–Signs

In order to begin this chapter there will be an overview of all three elements taken together and then separated and analyzed. These components make up the cultural–historical domain of Vygotsky's psychological–philosophical method.

According to Vygotsky, the actualization of human activity requires such intermediaries as *psychological tools* and the means of interpersonal communication.

> The concept of psychological tool arose first by loose analogy with the material tool that serves as a mediator between human hand and the object of action. Like material tools, psychological tools are artificial formations. By their nature, both are social. Whereas material tools are aimed at the control of the processes in nature, psychological tools master the natural behavioral and cognitive processes of the individual. Among the best known psychological tools, Vygotsky named sign and language systems, mnemonic techniques, and decision-making procedures that use such "tools," for example, dice. Unlike material tools, which serve as conductors of human influence on the objects of activity and which are, therefore, externally oriented, psychological tools are internally oriented, transforming natural human abilities and skills into higher mental functions. For example, if an elementary, natural memorizing effort connects event A with event B through the natural ability of the human brain, then in mnemonics this relation is replaced by two others: A to X and X to B, where X is an artificial psychological tool, such as a knot in a handkerchief, a written note, or a mnemonic scheme . . . (Kozulin, 1986, p. 266)

The relationship between the use of signs and tools can be subsumed under the heading of *mediated activity*, with the following understanding:

Mediated activity

Tool use   Sign use[51]

[51]See Vygotsky (1977, p. 71).

TOOLS

Before beginning it should be stated that the comparisons and differences between cognitive abilities of animals and humans will be left out; however, Vygotsky maintained that a fundamental behavior shared by both humans and animals is *signalization*.

> The fundamental and most general activity of the cerebral hemispheres in both man and animals is signalization; but the fundamental and most general activity distinguishing man from animals, psychologically speaking, is *signification*, i.e., the creation and use of signs. (Vygotsky, 1977, p. 62)

Therefore, before beginning this section a broader definition is given:

> signification: a person creates connections from without, and controls the brain, and through the brain, the body. The internal relation of functions and layers of the brain, as a fundamental regulatory principle in nervous activity, *is replaced* by social relations independent of the person and in the person (controlling the behavior of another) as a new regulatory principle. (Vygotsky, 1989, p. 63)

It is with this understanding in mind that we begin to define the interrelatedness of tools and signs within Vygotskian semiotics. Vygotsky was of the opinion that "signification represents one of man's artificial means of adaptation" (Vygotsky, 1977, p. 69), and with this understanding there are certain examples where signs can parallel the use of tools.

> The invention and use of signs as auxiliary means of solving a given psychological problem (to remember, compare something, report, choose, etc.) are analogous to the invention and use of tools in one, *psychological*, respect. The sign acts as an instrument of psychological activity in a manner analogous to the role of a tool in labor. (Vygotsky, 1977, pp. 69–70)

The assumption made is that *tools* and *signs* can be interrelated at points, however, it is important to initially view them as being separate. Vygotsky stated that "tools are outside the person; organs are within the person. The essence of intelligence lies in tools" (Vygotsky, 1989, p. 55). This point brings up the emergence of *consciousness* in Vygotskian understanding, which is then tied together with "tool" use:

> The essence of consciousness lies precisely in the knowledge of reality but is not confined to sensations, perceptions, representations and thought. It is also defined as being involved in the anticipation of events and actions, as having the quality of purposefulness (Spirkin, 1959). The emergence of consciousness is closely linked to the development of man's ability to use tools, that is a collective mastering of objects and

implements in an activity oriented towards his satisfaction of the primitive society. (Rahmani, 1973, p. 123)

There are many types of tools, such as technical tools, which serve as the intermediate link between human activity and the external object.[52] As well, there is the psychological tool, which directs mind and behavior, and the symbolic tool. Vygotsky warned against establishing parallels between material and psychological (also symbolic) tools, stating that "whereas in instrumental action the tool mediates human action directed at nature, in the symbolic act a psychological tool mediates man's own psychological processes" (Kozulin, 1990, p. 115). Meaningful activities within the higher mental functions are socially mediated at the beginning, and what actually transforms natural impulses into higher mental processes are the psychological tools used within mediation.

Psychological and Technical Tools

Before beginning this section, the following definition of tools and signs offered by Wertsch should be considered:

> Drawing on Marx (1977), he [Vygotsky] stated that a tool . . . serves as a conductor of humans' influence on the object of their activity. It is directed toward the external world . . . it is a means of humans' external activity; directed toward the subjugation of nature . . . In contrast to this external object orientation of a technical tool, Vygotsky argued that a sign [that is, a psychological tool] changes nothing in the object of a psychological operation. A sign is a means for psychologically influencing behavior . . . it is a means of internal activity, directed toward the mastery of humans themselves. A sign is inwardly directed . . . (Wertsch, 1985b, p. 78)

In general the psychological tool is not invented by the individual nor discovered in interaction with nature. The psychological tool does change the nature of mental functions, with an emphasis on transformation.[53] This transformation takes place within mediated activity, and basically mediated activity includes the following:

1. *Material tools*, which include collective orientation, interpersonal communication, and symbolic representation
2. *Psychological tools*, which mediate a human's own psychological processes

[52]See Kozulin (1990, p. 115).
[53]cf. Wertsch (1985b, pp. 79–80).

3. *Other human beings*, understood within the general genetic law of development, with this aspect being closely linked to the symbolic function.[54]

In actualizing human activity, psychological tools are needed to act as intermediaries, with psychological tools being used to regulate the cognitive processes of the individual, whereas material tools are employed in order to subjugate nature. Psychological tools are externally oriented, used in "transforming natural human abilities and skills into higher mental function" (Kozulin, 1986, p. 266). The example given is of tying a knot in a handkerchief to be used as an auxiliary means of future remembrance. Vygotsky viewed the introduction of a psychological tool (language, for example) into a mental function (such as memory) as causing a fundamental transformation of that function. "In his approach psychological tools are not viewed as auxiliary means that simply facilitate an existing mental function while leaving it qualitatively unaltered. Rather, the emphasis is on their capacity to transform mental functioning" (Wertsch, 1985b, p. 79). In 1930, Vygotsky and Luria outlined three points of importance in viewing the history of psychological tools, with

> anthropogenesis, the transformation of the natural intelligence of anthropoid apes into the "instrumental" intelligence of humans; the historical development of the "primitive" mind (*pensée sauvage*) into the modern one; and the ontogenetic development of the child's intelligence into its adult form" (Kozulin, 1984, p. 108).

Alex Kozulin has speculated on the importance of tools for Vygotsky, hypothesizing that his Jewish background might have played a significant role where religious objects serve as a reminder of the covenant. Some of these reminders are *phylacteries* (i.e., small leather boxes with leather laces attached, to be worn), and *tsitses* (i.e., tassels attached to the corners of garments).[55]

INTERNALIZATION

The most essential factor in forming the higher mental processes is internalization or interiorization. This idea was taken from Karl Bühler, and was of course developed differently by Piaget. For Vygotsky,

> (1) internalization is not a process of copying external reality on a preexisting internal plane; rather, it is a process wherein an internal plane of consciousness is formed. (2) The external reality at issue is a social interactional one. (3) The specific mechanism at issue is the mastery of external sign forms. And (4) the internal plane of consciousness takes on a "quasi-social" nature because of its origins (Wertsch, 1985a, p. 67).

[54]cf. Kozulin & Presseisen (1995, pp. 67–70).
[55]Kozulin (1984, p. 136).

It is important to remember that the process of internalization is not automatic and matures only through a long series of developmental events. One of the challenging aspects in focusing on *action to thought* is the concept of *internalized meaning*. David Bakhurst has stated the problem succinctly: "Vygotsky is challenging: that meaning can only be understood as a special property of mental objects" (Bakhurst, 1991, p. 81). One of the problems that might arise with this view is the lack of objectivity in research experiments, which has been addressed by Bakhurst (1991) in a footnote:

> This led Vygotsky to the idea that psychological development can sometimes best be studied if the analist actively intervenes in that development by, for example, offering subjects new psychological tools with which to undertake operations under investigation . . . or engaging subjects in activities thought to precipitate internalization, so as to observe the relationship among (a) what subjects can achieve unaided, (b) what they can achieve when assisted by others, and (c) the trajectory of their subsequent development . . . (p. 83)

In many of his experiments, Vygotsky attempted to study both verbal meaning and play in their natural surroundings, which encouraged much criticism of his research techniques, labeling him a representative of *cultural relativism* and *mentalism*.[56] Vygotsky was not totally interested in a psychology of action, but in one of mental processes, and "in order to realize the dynamic functional role of the acquired verbal meanings, we have to switch over from the genetic plane to the functional plane, and what we have to study is not the development of meanings and the changes in their structure, but the process of how the meanings function in living, verbal thought" (Vari-Szilagyi, 1991, p. 113). In defining *meaning*, Vygotsky stated that

> Each word has meaning . . . *Meaning does not coincide with logical meaning* (nonsense has meaning) . . . the constant claim in all authors: the meaning of all words is fixed, meaning does not develop . . . "*Meaning is the path from the thought to the word*". . . . <Meaning is not the sum of all the psychological operations which stand behind the word> Meaning is something more specific—it is the internal structure of the sign operation. It is what is lying between the thought and the word. Meaning is not equal to the word, not equal to the thought. (Vygotsky in Rieber & Wollock, 1997, pp. 132–133 [not published during Vygotsky's life. Notes found in the private archives of A. N. Leontiev])

V. P. Zinchenko has given a critique of Vygotsky's understanding of meaning by claiming that it cannot be viewed as "a universally or genetically primary unit for the analysis of mind" (Zinchenko, 1985a, p. 100). Therefore, Zinchenko is of the opinion that *word meaning* cannot be used as a unit of analysis. During the 1920s Bakhtin and Mandel'shtam [Mandelstam] both introduced an extended term with the concept of "object meaning," with Holzkamp reintroducing this idea in the

---

[56]For a more detailed discussion, see Vari-Szilagyi (1991, p. 115).

1970s. The inclusion of object meaning was to allow the subject's experience to be instantiated in practical activity. At this point, Zinchenko stated that "internalization is the activity–semiotic transformation not of tools, but of their meanings . . . In addition . . . the idea that tool-mediated action can function as a unit for the analysis of mind was not distinctly articulated by anyone" (Zinchenko, 1985b, pp. 100–103). At this point it is important to understand that a concise discussion of *tools* and *psychological tools* is most difficult to undertake because of the diffuse nature of the topic. However, one of the major differences in Vygotsky and the Russian School of *activity theory* was the fact that Vygotsky was known to frequently speak in *metaphors*, and often these metaphors were interpreted *literally* by some of his followers. In fact, the entire concept of *internalization* or *interiorization* is also seen by some as being a metaphor itself.[57] After Vygotsky's death the followers of *activity theory*, for the most part, eliminated *semiotic mediation* from their research and writings, primarily because of its abstractness.

> Alexey Alexeevich Leontiev (son of A.N. Leontiev) took up this discussion during the 1960s and later in his writings on psycholinguistics by actually bridging Vygotsky's understanding of signs with his father's activity theory.

Vygotsky understood the genesis of signs "as a process of internalizing the means of social communication" (Rahmani, 1973, p. 41), demonstrating the importance of the social as the initial starting point of semiotics. The stages of internalization are the natural or preintellectual stage, the stage of naive psychology, the stage of egocentric speech, and the so-called ingrowth stage (cf. Emerson, 1996, p. 131). Without going into an in-depth discussion of these stages, it should be understood that there is not a dualistic fallacy regarding the internalization of social practices. In other words, via mediation, internalization is the center stage where transformations take place. Within the framework of the dialectic, and moving continuously from whole to part to whole (as well as from part to whole to part), a very important point is made by Vygotsky: *internalization is a metaphorical mechanism that does not remain static*. Without an inclusion of dialectical principles, misunderstandings quickly arise, such as the problem of speech and thought maintaining separate origins. An example would be to use a statement of Vygotsky regarding the vocal and semantic aspects of speech (which metaphorically parallels the problems of externalization/internalization): "Since they move in opposite directions, their development does not coincide; but that does not mean that they are independent of each other. On the contrary, their difference is the first stage of a close union" (Vygotsky, 1994a, p. 219). It is with this dynamic state of development in mind that we enter the discussion of signs.

---

[57]"It is stressed that the interiorization process is not merely a move of a function from without, but rather the process of building the inner (mental) structure of consciousness. The word 'interiorization' should be thus considered as a metaphor depicting the result rather than the process of development of higher psychological functions" (Aidman & Leontiev, 1991, p. 143).

SIGNS

> The sign . . . changes nothing in the object of a psychological operation. It is a means
> of internal activity aimed at mastering man himself; the sign is *internally* oriented.
> These activities are so different from each other that the nature of the means they use
> cannot be the same in both cases. (Vygotsky, 1977, p. 72)

Signs are ultimately used for self-regulation and human beings cannot function at the level of higher psychological processes without continuous use of
signs, which mediate communication. Signs require an intermediary link between
unconditioned *stimulus and response* mechanisms,[58] which refer to *speech*
brought into the operation, fulfilling a special function. With speech, there is an
automatic breaking away from the biological development with the potential
of creating higher levels of cultural development. For this to happen there needs
to be a dialectical relationship of reversal in place, where words can serve the
function of both stimulus and response.

> Vygotsky focused upon language as a mediating device, rather than such isolated
> semiotic devices as the aforementioned knot used as mnemonic aids because language
> is a system of *reversible* signs organized in terms of principles of multifunctionality,
> communication, and generalization. (Lee in Wertsch, 1985a, p. 76)

Language is the focus of attention at this stage, because "it is the only sign
system that can refer to itself" (Lee in Wertsch, 1985a, pp. 76–77). Signs are
not passed down to future generations in the way genes are, which implies that
semiotic and cultural systems can be lost if not nurtured and carried on by future
generations. For example, in the beginning of ontogenetic development the child
does not comprehend the connection between sign and meaning, which is social
in origin and which is imposed by adults and caregivers, later being internalized
by the child.

> . . . The fact that at their first stages the higher psychological functions are built as
> outer forms of behavior and find support in the outer sign is by no means accidental;
> on the contrary, it is determined by the very psychological nature as a direct continu-
> ation of elementary processes but is a *social method of behaviour applied by itself to
> itself*. (Vygotsky, 1994, p. 153)

With the process of internalization, the lower preceding levels of development remain in their core form; however, a qualitative change results in new psychological processes, with new functional needs. Vygotsky listed various speech
functions, which can be categorized in oppositional pairs, but are not to be
equated with intra-intermental planes of functioning.

---

[58] In private communication, Leo van Lier (1998) stated that the old understanding of "stimulus and
response" should be abandoned in favor of an ecological framework. In fact Vygotsky's entire semiotic structure could be rewritten within a richer context of ecology.

signaling function	vs.	significative function
social function	vs.	individual function
communicative function	vs.	intellectual function
indicative function	vs.	symbolic function

(cf. Wertsch, 1985b)

These oppositions do not all play equally important roles in Vygotsky's semiotic analysis. Rather, they can be divided into two categories. The first three oppositions deal with the mediation of social and psychological processes at a fairly general level of analysis and have little to say about the specifics of the signs involved. In contrast, the indicative and symbolic functions are defined in terms of specific relationships that exist between signs and extralinguistic reality and between signs and other signs. (Wertsch, 1985b, p. 89)

In order to specify these functions in further detail, the following can be said:

1. The signaling function is based on Pavlov's understanding of reflexes and the second signal system of speech; however, Vygotsky went beyond this understanding with his descriptions of these functions.
2. The "distinction between the social and individual functions of speech is a distinction between mediational means for interpsychological and intrapsychological functions, respectively,"[59] which directly views adult directives or commands used in order to regulate child behavior.
3. "A major concern for Vygotsky when analyzing the communicative and intellectual functions of speech was that their inherent and necessary interconnection be recognized"[60] (Wertsch, 1985b, p. 94)
4. The indicative vs. symbolic function describes the development from pointing and gesturing to symbolic functions, all of which incorporates both concrete and abstract thinking to various degrees. Any mediated action involves an "irreducible tension, or dialectic, between mediational means, on the one hand, and their unique use by an individual or individuals, on the other hand."

Within the context of Vygotsky's thought during the 1920s, it is clear that his main interest was in the development of higher, cultural realms, which would be available to the individual to express his/her highest potential. In understanding cultural–historical theory Vygotsky emphasized the emergence and change of psychological tools, of which language was of primary concern. When the use of speech and thought "begin to interweave in action, a dialectic is set up in which the reversible nature of signs allows the child to 'bootstrap' himself up through the various levels of abstraction present in language" (Lee in Wertsch, 1985a,

[59]Wertsch (1985b, p. 92).
[60]Ibid., p. 94.

p. 79). The entire framework being described is surrounded by the social field, which includes change and development, much of which has been left out of the structuralist–linguistic framework of de Saussure, for example.[61]

In concluding the thoughts on *tools–psychological tools–internalization or interiorization–signs*, Vygotsky stated that in certain instances tools and signs were used analogously; however, this analogy does not imply an isomorphic identity between the two.

> The invention and use of signs as auxiliary means of solving a given psychological problem (to remember, compare something, report, choose, etc.) are analogous to the invention and use of tools in one, *psychological* respect. The sign acts as an instrument of psychological activity in a manner analogous to the role of a tool in labor. (Vygotsky, 1977, p. 70)

HISTORY

A basic understanding of Vygotsky's concept of history is important, because it represents a centerpiece of his psychology–philosophy. Singling out general history as the foundation for the entire theoretical edifice seems consistent with Vygotsky's own view of his enterprise. He begins *The Development of Higher Mental Functions* with a quotation from Engels: "The eternal laws of nature to an ever greater extent are changing into laws of history" (Scribner, 1985, p. 121). Traditionally, there has been a conceptually infelicitous *side-taking* with certain scholars emphasizing Vygotsky's theory as a *cultural historical theory* (i.e., Davydov & Radzikhovskii), and another approach called *Soviet sociohistorical approach* (e.g., A. N. Leontiev & Luria). "In contrast to phylogenesis, in which the line of historical–cultural development *displaces* the biological, in ontogenesis both lines of development co-occur and are fused" (Scribner, 1997, p. 246). Vygotsky viewed history within a functionalist and dialectical perspective, studying *phenomena in movement*; in fact "the essence of a dialectical approach . . . is to study something historically" (Scribner, 1985, p. 120). The question then asked is, What are historical laws? Vygotsky gave an overview of the approach taken by several schools of psychology regarding the relationship of history and psychology, concluding that "it is not enough to formally bring psychology and history closer to one another; it is necessary to ask: what psychology and what history are we dealing with?" (Scribner, 1985, p. 122). History for Vygotsky was the starting point of understanding between both the *child* and the *primitive,* yet history was not understood or explained within the constant

---

[61]". . . As writers from the Prague Linguistic Circle . . . to the present day . . . have noted, the structuralist focus on synchrony, langue, and abstract universal competence, has tended to obscure the importance both of language change and development, and of the particularities of socio-cultural process" (Sinha, 1988, p. 100).

parameters of stability. In viewing history within his lifetime, Vygotsky did not feel that the conceptual thinking of his time was superior to times past, yet he felt that he was standing at a historic moment where societal change was taking place from moment to moment. His frantic pace of living testifies to the belief that he was helping shape history. In general, Vygotsky's understanding of history was distributed within the genetic domains of phlyogeny, ontogeny, the cultural–historical or sociocultural, and the microgenetic lineage.

Sylvia Scribner described Vygotsky's understanding of the role of history within the various genetic domains, beginning with what she labeled *general history* or the first level of history. Here she stated that "for Vygotsky . . . the transformation of phylogeny (biological evolution) into general history (historical development) is more than a backdrop for a Marxist psychology" (Scribner, 1997, pp. 245–246). In beginning with phylogeny, Scribner only mentioned Vygotsky's understanding of animals; however, some of his views are worth stating. To begin the discussion within the phylogenetic plane, it is confusing to follow some of the debates on whether Vygotsky felt that human development was a continuation of higher animal development or not, or if Vygotsky felt that young children's thinking parallels the cognitive abilities of higher animals. First of all, it is important to understand that Vygotsky's philosophy was partly based on the tenets of Spinoza, who was a 17th century Dutch Jewish philosopher. As we have seen, Spinoza was a monist and wrote in part to counteract the "mind–body" dualism of Descartes, which *inter alia* positioned man in a higher relationship to animals. This positioning was not the same for Spinoza. It is important to understand the overall context of Vygotsky's ultimate respect for the animal world; indeed he suggested that tests be given to higher animals, without expecting them to use speech, so that humans might learn to appreciate the value and high level of communication of which animals are capable.[62] In other quotes he stated aspects such as the following: "Human behavior differs qualitatively from animal behavior to the same extent that the adaptability and historical development of humans differ from the adaptability and development of animals" (Vygotsky, 1978, p. 60). Vygotsky felt that animal behavior is influenced by both innate reactions and "conditioned reflexes (which were themselves combinations of innate reactions and personal experience)" (van der Veer & Valsiner, 1991, p. 51). In contrast, he viewed human behavior being characterized by: (1). Innate characteristics, (2). Conditioned reflexes, (3). History, (4). Social experience, (5). "Doubled experience" (van der Veer & Valsiner, 1991, p. 52), with the double experience referring to the *general genetic law of cultural development*. Wolfgang Köhler asked the question whether anthropoids have the same capacity of developing parts of their intellect such as man. Vygotsky concluded with Köhler that the answer is yes, meaning that intellect and language capacity function apart

---

[62]See Vygotsky (1994a, pp. 70–71).

from each other up to a certain point.[63] Vygotsky determined that one of the connecting links between animals and humans was within the realm of emotions.[64] Indeed there were superficial conflicts of statements made by Vygotsky regarding the comparison of "tool use" of preverbal children to apes. The second level of history discussed by Scribner related to ontogeny. It is here that the question is asked whether ontogeny recapitulates phylogeny. "Just as Vygotsky rejected the notion that biological laws can explain the emergence of higher forms of behavior in general history, he rejected their explanatory value for these behaviors in child history as well" (Scribner, 1985, p. 246). Before giving examples of various positions on this issue, a general problem has been stated by Gould (1977) in Scribner (Wertsch, 1985a, pp. 127–128). Although the overall concept of ontogeny represents the entire lifespan of the individual, conventionally only development up to adulthood is normally considered in most research. As well, Scribner pointed out that general comparisons between ontogeny and phylogeny often take immature members of a higher species and compare them with mature members of the lower species.

In returning to the problem of Vygotsky's position regarding ontogeny repeating phylogeny, "Vygotsky vigorously denies that his is either a recapitulationist or a parallelist position" (Scribner, 1985, p. 129). However, David Bakhurst (1991) expressed a more extended opinion when stating the following: "I believe that Vygotsky did think that there was an important symmetry between ontogenesis and phylogenesis, between the development of the individual and the development of the human race. However, he [Vygotsky] denied (against Hall) that the repetition of phylogenesis in ontogenesis was a matter of *biological* inheritance, that the child's development is conditioned by an inherited causal process defined by the course of evolutionary development of the species" (p. 129). Other authors such as David Joravsky (1987) state that "Vygotskii [Vygotsky] dreamed of a psychological analogue to the 'biogenetic' law that ontogeny recapitulates phylogeny" (p. 204). What makes this issue so volatile has been the misuse of recapitulation theory to support racist ideology within various countries. The third line of history is that of the higher psychological processes–functions. As opposed to many psychologists, Vygotsky did not offer a *progression of cultural devel-*

[63]The question arises as to whether humans actually descended from animals, with those disagreeing forming a consensus for the "critical point" theory. There is discussion of this in Bakhurst (1991, p. 74), and in van der Veer & Valsiner (1991, p 199). The latter writers state that "To say that biological evolution and human history did not overlap is, a theory that claims that the development of the capacity for acquiring culture was a sudden occurrence in the phylogeny of primates. Accepting this now discredited view (Geertz, 1973, pp. 62–69) involves in essence seeing biological development as the precursor of cultural development. It does not seem that Engels' and Vygotsky's theory implied such a point of view." There is confusion in the literature as to what Vygotsky actually thought, however it appears that he did not use man's capacity of language to place humans at a higher level than animals.

[64]See Vygotsky's article "Emotions and their development" in Rieber (1987, pp. 325–337).

opmental stages, and as well, he also did not offer levels of progressions within higher mental functions. He was interested in the functional systems of the higher mental processes and not so much interested in establishing cognitive levels of intelligence. Scribner also pointed out the interesting fact that in his overall understanding of experimentation, Vygotsky worked with adults in industrialized Russia, as well as adults in more primitive settings in Siberia, also working with mentally challenged children. Vygotsky's ideas concerning history are not free of controversy; however, his approach was a call to

> look to cultural history for hypotheses about the origin and transformation of higher functional systems. His work may be read as an attempt to weave three strands of history—general history, child history, and the history of mental functions—into one explanatory account of the formation of specifically human aspects of human nature. (Scribner, 1997, p. 258)

It is suggested that the most important aspect regarding Vygotsky's understanding of history was its parallel meaning as an agent for societal and personal change.

THOUGHT–WORD–WORD MEANINGS–LANGUAGE

When looking up books in university libraries in the United States with the title words *thought* and *language*, an interesting phenomenon occurs. Out of the usual first 50 titles it becomes obvious that with very few exceptions authors from the West will normally start with the word *language*, while Slavic authors often begin with the word *thought*. Vygotsky became intrigued with these words after reading A. A. Potebnya's book titled *Thought and Language*. Two concepts from this book had a great impact on Vygotsky, namely *word* and *image*:

> According to Potebnya, "Originally every word consists of three elements: the unity of articulated sounds, i.e., the *external sign* of signification; representation, i.e., the *internal sign* of signification; and *signification* itself. . . . By "signification" Potebnya means the image of an object expressed in words . . . "representation" plays the role of a substitute for an object's sensory image, realized in words as its "inner form." The inner form of a word is, in turn, an image unrelated to the word, but its "essential" . . . Thus, the imagistic nature of a word . . . represented by its "essential" attribute are not absolutely arbitrary. (Kharitonov, 1991a, pp. 10–11)

In this quote the influence of Humboldt's *inner form* is evident, as well as the focus on *image*. Potebnya used heuristics as his guiding principle, all of which was framed within poetry and literature. He wrote metaphorically, stating thoughts such as, "the word as such does not have a thought in it, but is only its 'imprint,'" which under certain conditions ". . . produces in the listener a process of thought creation similar to what had just taken place in the speaker."[65] For Potebnya *word* is not the same for the speaker as for the listener, basing this on Humboldt's thesis that "all understanding is at the same time misunderstanding" (Kharitonov, 1991a, p. 11). The focus was not to simply understand single words, but to understand words in uttered speech, within a context. In understanding an important point regarding the range of influence Potebnya had on Vygotsky, one needs to begin with the role of *image*:

> "All significations in language are imagistic in origin." "Every word, like every pho-
> netic sign of signification, is based on a combination of sound and meaning that is
> either simultaneous or successive, and consequently is a metaphor" . . . Hence, Poteb-
> nya concludes that a poetic image is always an allegory, in the broad sense of the word.
> (Kharitonov, 1991a, p. 14)

In going beyond the *word*, the basic understanding in verbal communica-
tion is *dialogue*, which is represented as a whole with two components, speech and comprehension. "To use Potebnya's terms, comprehension becomes possible if the image is more known than the object it describes, explains, or replaces" (Kharitonov, 1991, p. 7).

Vygotsky has come to be known by his use of *word* in his semiotics and not *sentence*. However, the meaningful *word* is always understood contextually by Vygotsky, never on its own, and it is hypothesized that many of his thoughts on *word* were written from a metaphorical stance, rather than as a scientific fact. Vygotsky viewed *word* from a functional perspective, borrowing some of his ideas from Pierre Janet; for example, "the functions of a word according to Janet were first divided and distributed among people, and then became part of the person. Nothing similar could exist in individual consciousness and behavior" (Vygotsky, 1989, p. 61). Even before the work of Janet, one of the first Russian linguists to develop the idea of *the functional structure of the word* was G. G. Shpet (Spět), where the external and internal form were distinguished.[66] And as well, A. A. Potebnya wrote specifically about the *word*, which he not only viewed as being a sign, but also a tool *capable of converting concrete images into abstract concepts.*[67] It is stated that the key to higher behavior is within *sociogenesis* (a composite of the four domains, including phylogenesis, ontogenesis, cultural–historical or sociocultural development, and microgenesis), thereby placing the *psychological* (not biological) function of the *word* at the center of Vygotsky's understanding. Scholars have not been able to completely agree on what Vygotsky actually meant by *word*. James Wertsch, as well as Ingrid Rissom (writing in German),[68] have stated that for Vygotsky the *word* actually refers to *speech*:

[65]Kharitonov (1991a, p. 12).
[66]See Davydov & Zinchenko (1993, p. 96).
[67]See Ladislav Matejka (1978 [1980], p. 146).
[68]"Vygotskij [Vygotsky] verwendet in diesem Zusammenhang den Terminus *slovo*, den im engen
    wörtlichen Sinne als *Wort* zu übersetzen insofern unglücklich ist, als Vygotskij [Vygotsky] hier nicht

> ... [Herein] Vygotsky consistently uses the term *word* [*slovo*] where it may appear
> ... that *speech* [*rech*] would be more appropriate. Since Vygotsky's emphasis here is
> on how signs mediate social and individual activity rather than on the process of speech
> activity, it would seem that his use of *word* rather than *speech* is significant ... It
> should be noted ... that one should not take the term *word* too literally. Since it is used
> in connection with Vygotsky's general concern with sign mediation, it does not refer
> solely to morphological units; rather, phrases, sentences, and entire texts fall under this
> category as well. (Wertsch, 1981, p. 158)

In trying to assume an approximation of Vygotsky's understanding and use of *word*, it is hypothesized that his cultural, poetic, literary, theatrical, and other influences led him to return to the source of creativity, which was the *word*. It is further assumed that Vygotsky's *genetic–development* approach afforded him with an understanding of the *word* as a starting point for creative exploration, as well as serving as a vehicle for transforming and developing *imaginistic* thoughts, which were then completed in the *word*. As P. Tulviste has stated, there are very few articles written on Vygotsky's aesthetics by well-known or even unknown scholars in the West, and this aspect of the arts was one of the most important influences in Vygotsky's life.[69] It is suggested that the *word* for Vygotsky represented the *essence* of art and later that of psychology on a metaphorical level. Vygotsky's childhood friend, S. Dobkin stated that Lev Semonovich from his youth until his last days loved to recite poetry. "To him, the opening words were sufficient for grasping the essence" (Dobkin, 1982, p. 27). In understanding the positioning of the *word* in Russian literature in general, Roman Jakobson, who studied in Moscow at the same time Vygotsky did, stated the following:

> The term slovesnost (derived from *slovo* "the word"), which is still used in Russian to
> designate literature as an object of study and which solidly ties it to the "word," prop-
> erly characterizes this tendency. The term is especially useful with respect to the oral
> tradition. (Jakobson & Pomorska, 1983, p. 10)

In returning to an analysis of the *word*, its first function for Vygotsky is social,[70] and according to Janet the *word* was initially used to command others. It then went through a complex history of changes; "Therefore, if we want to clarify genetically the origins of the voluntary function of the word and why the word overrides motor responses, we must inevitably arrive at the real function

---

auf das Wort als Teileinheit innerhalb eines Satzes, sondern auf die einzelne sprachliche Äußerung abhebt; parallel dazu spricht Vygotskij [Vygotsky] auch von *mysl, Gedanke*, womit der jeweils besondere Denkprozeß und nicht die Denktätigkeit im allgemeinen bezeichnet wird" (Rissom, 1985, p. 310). Translation: In this connection Vygotsky used the term *slovo*, which is unfortunate when translated in the narrow, literal sense of *word*; Vygotsky did not refer to the *word* as a partial unit within a sentence, but rather to a single linguistic sentence/or utterance; at the same time, Vygotsky spoke of *mysl, thought*, where accordingly a respective thought process was characterized, not [gen-eralized] thinking ability. [DR]

[69]See P. Tul'viste [Tulviste], *Soviet Psychology* (1989a, Vol. 27/2, pp. 37–52).

[70]See Vygotsky (1981, p. 158).

of commanding in both ontogenesis and phylogenesis" (Vygotsky, 1981, pp. 158–159). Vygotsky did not want to impart the understanding that human knowledge was created through the *word* only—what he was attempting is the following: ". . . Vygotsky transforms Von Humboldt's emphasis on the word's inner form into a site in which the interaction between language and thought can be studied" (Burgess, 1993, p. 24). A word refers to a group or class of objects and is a generalization, which means that *words* are not natural but must be constructed.[71] Now, a misunderstanding could easily arise with the assumption that Vygotsky wanted the *word* to be the basic component of "living speech," which is not the case. Luria offered his understanding on this point:

> It is precisely this that has led many psychologists and linguists (e.g., Humboldt, 1905, 1907; de Saussure, 1922; and the Russian linguist Potebnya, 1888) to argue that it is not the word but the *sentence* which constitutes the basic unit of living speech. As we shall see, simply naming something, without formulating a thought or idea, is quite artificial, whereas the expression of a complete thought or the formulation of an idea is the basic unit of communication. Thus, we may assert that *if the word is the element of language, the sentence is the unit of living speech.* (Luria, 1981, p. 116)

At this point there is a putative similarity between the Western and Russian understanding of the *sentence*, which could be deceiving. In order to avoid any confusion, an example from Bakhtin will be given as being representative of the general Russian linguistic perspective:

> When Bakhtin discusses "problems of syntax," he has in mind the utterance as it occurs in context, in lived social time. Hence that object of study has rather fluid, generically determined boundaries, ranging from utterances consisting of a single word to utterances consisting of the entire text of a literary work. (Stewart, 1983, p. 267)

Because *words* are generalizations, not just categories, *thoughts* must then be viewed as having separate functions as well. Vygotsky (Rieber & Wollock, 1997) stated that:

> The thought also has independent existence; it does not coincide with the meanings. *We have to find a certain construction of the meanings in order to be able to express a thought* [text and ulterior motive] . . . "*The thought is completed in the word.*" . . . The process of the realization of the thought in meaning is a complex phenomenon which proceeds inward "from motives to speaking." . . . (p. 135)

Vygotsky wrote that there are two distinct lines of initial development in the child, which include a prelinguistic understanding in thought and a preintellectual understanding in speech; however, this understanding has been rejected by many Russian psychologists (stating that the origin of thought and language is labor).[72] The question arises as to when speech becomes meaningful, and Vygotsky (in Bakhurst, 1986) stated that

---

[71]See Daniels (1993, pp. 24–25).

[72]Průcha (1972, p. 14) stated: "This concept of different genetic roots of thought and speech has been rejected in Soviet psychology, and the existence of prelinguistic thought and preintellectual

> The most significant moment in the course of intellectual development, which gives
> birth to the purely human forms of practical and abstract intelligence, occurs when
> speech and practical activity, two previously completely independent lines of devel-
> opment, converge. (p. 115)

With a long process of *engagements* and *separations*,[73] the line of development continues until speech assumes the same role that parallels *tool* in
problem-solving activity, and there is never a constant level of meaning or understanding that results from this discovery. It should be mentioned that the last lines
of some of the last works to be published by Vygotsky returned to metaphorical
speech, using the concept of the single *word.* "Consciousness is reflected in a
word as the sun in a drop of water."[74] In Western understanding, *word* appears to
be a single unit, alone, without context. It represents the "bare-bones" approach
to a unified linguistics. This is not the feel from a Humboldtian perspective,
with the paradoxical thought that "in reality speech is not assembled from
pre-existing words. On the contrary, words come from the totality of speech"
(Basilius, 1952, p. 100).

WORD MEANING AND SENSE

The reason Vygotsky selected *word meaning as a unit of analysis* was to
understand the relationship between *thought* and *speech.* Word meaning was
viewed as the unit, which maintained the properties of the whole connecting both
thought and speech. There is not a one-to-one fit within thought and speech and
the relationship between them stands in an asymmetrical, dynamic process of
change. Word meaning is situated in history and does not remain constant;
however, word meaning also serves another purpose. "It may be appropriate to
view word meaning not only as *a unity of thinking and speech*, but as a *unity of
generalization and social interaction, a unity of thinking and communication*"

speech has not been recognized, as it is generally believed that thought may have its origin only in
speech." There was a man named Kolbanovsky, who must have defended Vygotsky in Party meet-
ings and at other occasions. He was one of the first to introduce Vygotsky to new readers in 1956.
Kolbanovsky did state to Party officials that Vygotsky had made a mistake: "Likewise, it was the
younger Vygotsky who had claimed erroneously that speech and thinking have different roots:
speech and thinking could not have different roots as Engels (1925) had clearly demonstrated that
both originated in practical labor activity" (van der Veer & Valsiner, 1991, p. 384). What is interesting about the rejection of the two lines of development is that with Vygotsky's argument: "Intellect and speech have different genetic roots and they have developed along different lines. There is
no fixed correlation between their development in phylogenesis. Anthropoid apes display an intellect resembling that of humans in certain respects (such as the use of tools), while their 'language'
resembles human speech in a quite different respect ..." (Vygotsky quoted in Kozulin, 1990,
p. 152).

[73]For a discussion on *separations* and *engagements*, refer to Kozulin (1990, p. 157).
[74]Vygotsky quoted in Kozulin (1994, p. 256).

(Minick, 1996, p. 40). Word meaning cannot be understood without being a *generalization* and *an abstraction*; as well, the communicative function of speech cannot be divorced from the intellectual function when viewing the development of word meaning.[75]

In Vygotskian terminology there is a difference between *meaning* and *sense*, with *meaning* possessing a general, widely accepted understanding, such as is found in a dictionary. *Sense*, on the other hand, differs with each individual and also over time; "the sense of a word is the sum of all the psychological events aroused in a person's consciousness by the word. It is dynamic, complex, fluid, whole, which has several zones of unequal stability. Meaning is only one of the zones of sense, and the most stable and precise zone" (Kozulin, 1994, p. xxxvii). Vygotsky drew on the work of Paulhan by implying that *meaning* is ". . . the dictionary style of definition of the concept, while 'sense' represents the sum of psychological events aroused in consciousness by word. While the former is said always to remain constant, the latter is in a state of constant flux" (Bakhurst, 1986, p. 121). This dichotomy can be used for a better understanding of the true complexity regarding simple lexical associations between teachers and learners, learners and learners, and so forth. In a footnote, A. A. Leontiev and Wertsch stated that:

> Meaning is a property of a sign. Sense is the content of meaning (the result of meaning), but is not fixed in the sign (Vygotsky, 1968, p. 193). [In Vygotsky's book *Thought and Language* (Cambridge, Mass.: MIT Press, 1962), the Russian word *smysl* has been interpreted as "sense," and *znachenie*, as "meaning" . . . However, it is worth noting that the term *meaning* in Soviet psychology is virtually synonymous with the term *sense* for Frege. The term *sense* as used in Soviet psychology is much more difficult to analyze in terms familiar to an American reader.—J. W.]. (Wertsch, 1978, p. 20)

Vygotsky stated simply that "to understand another's speech, it is not sufficient to understand his words—we must understand his thought" (Vygotsky, 1994a, p. 253), which was an attempt to take analysis to the *innermost plane*. It is at this point that "word/word meaning" form a whole, just as thought/language, within a dialectical framework. For example:

> "Word" represents the external side of "word meaning," with both WORD and WORD MEANING forming a dynamic, dialectical unity. "Word meaning" is then comprehended by "inner speech," which can be divided into "meaning" (the stabilized, conventional understanding among many peoples) and "sense" (which is the less stable, dynamic–developmental side of human interpretation). Word meaning, derived from inner speech, is broken down into "meaning" and "sense," which also incorporates a subjective side including emotions, motivation, volition . . . Vygotsky stated that "a true and full understanding of another's thought is possible only when we understand its affective–volitional basis." (Vygotsky, 1994a, p. 252)

[75]Following the thoughts of N. J. Minick in Daniels (1996, p. 40).

Therefore, *word* is positioned within *thought* and *speech* functioning in a dialectical fashion, and

> if word meanings change in their inner nature, then the relation of thought to word also changes. To understand the dynamics of that relation, we must supplement the genetic approach of our main study by functional analysis and examine the role of word meaning in the process of thought. (Vygotsky, 1994a, p. 217)

Thought does not produce thought; motives, emotions, needs, interests, desires, and so on actually engender thoughts. Vygotsky introduced a most important continuum: in speaking the child starts off from words (parts) to sentences (whole); however, in grasping the meaning of what is being stated by others, the opposite then occurs with the child going from semantics (whole) to words (parts), all of which demonstrate that the development of these two lines of speech and thought are genetically different, yet function together. Vygotsky would say that "thought and word are not cut from one pattern."[76]

> If word meanings change in their inner nature, then the relation of thought to word also changes. To understand the dynamics of that relation, we must supplement the genetic approach of our main study by functional analysis and examine the role of word meaning in the process of thought. (Vygotsky, 1994a, p. 217)

Vygotsky's understanding of the development of the *word* must then accompany the function of the *word* in communication;[77] and with the co-extensive array of *word meaning* (including meaning and sense), Vygotsky tells us that *thought and speech turn out to be the key to the nature of human consciousness.* Word meaning is used to comprehend dialectical, internal relationships, and the reason Vygotsky used *word meaning* as his basic "unit of analysis" was to establish a procedure which could be implemented in comprehending the smallest components, all of which, unlike elements, retain all of the basic properties of the whole and which cannot be further divided without losing them (cf. Bakhurst, 1986, p. 110). There is the famous example of H_2O where hydrogen burns, while oxygen sustains fire, demonstrating that the analysis of the properties of these elements alone cannot afford a correct synthesis of the properties of water.[78]

---

[76]Vygotsky (1994a, p. 219).

[77]See Minick (1987, p. 26).

[78]Vygotsky has been criticized on numerous occasions for his account of units and elements. Here is a quote regarding the comparison of Vygotsky and another well-known Russian psychologist: "Vygotsky overlooked the *structural-qualitative* nature of Basov's separation of . . . the 'real, objective elements' . . . of psychological processes. Instead, Vygotsky considered the 'differential elements' . . . to be 'real elements,' and reiterates Basov's call for structural analysis of relationships of these elements in dynamically organized processes. However . . . *Basov emphasized the use of exactly the opposite kinds of unit . . . qualitatively different sub-components . . . which make up . . . a qualitatively new structure* . . . Basov followed Köhler's separation of 'real' and 'differential' elements, whereas Vygotsky mixed the two kinds up by displacing the meaning of the latter . . . as if it belonged to the former . . ." (Valsiner, 1988, pp. 27–32).

Vygotsky was actually referring to the internal side of *word meaning* in order to establish a whole unit, with the external structure of *word* completing it. *Word meaning* can be distinguished by two features: "these are the meaning of the expression in the true sense of the word and its function as a name which relates to a particular object, that is, its object relatedness" (Vygotsky in Rieber, 1987, p. 152). Then the question is raised as to whether *word meaning* is speech or thought. In reality it is both at the same time. It is easy to establish the correspondence between *word meaning* and *word*, but a *word* is also related to an entire group of a class of objects, not to a single object; therefore it is a generalization, and as such is a *verbal act of thought* (cf. Vygotsky, 1987, p. 47). Generally speaking, *word meaning* is both a unit of thinking and social interaction and cannot be understood if divorced from communicative and intellectual functions.[79]

INNER SPEECH

Inner speech is not simply internal talking; it is a function in its own right. It has been asked why egocentric speech turns to inner speech and the reason is that the function or functional needs change. "Egocentric speech occurs when the child begins to differentiate the representational aspects of speech from its pragmatic communicative functions. Language used to represent the means–end and interpersonal aspects of communicative interactions leads to the development of "inner speech" and linguistically mediated motivation" (Wertsch, 1985a, pp. 82–83). Vygotsky's interpretation of inner speech originally went back to Humboldt's *inner form*, placing it in the context of the work of Kurt Goldstein. Going beyond Goldstein, Vygotsky wrote about dialectical transformations of speech including the external and internal form, all of which were understood to be socially organized.[80]

For Vygotsky, inner speech maintains its own syntactic and semantic features. In other words,

> For Vygotsky *inner speech* is a particular, independent aspect of verbal thought in which all the dynamic relations between thought and words are concentrated. This is speech in and for itself. It emerges from external speech and differs from it by being maximally abbreviated. (Akhutina, 1978, p. 14)

The basic components of inner speech are

1. Its predicative nature. For example, the subject of our thoughts is always understood and is then abbreviated.
2. The phonetic aspect is diminished. Pronouncing a word in its entirety is unnecessary.

[79]See Rieber (1987, pp. 27–32).
[80]See van der Veer & Valsiner (1991, p. 179).

3. It maintains a semantic structure of its own and the properties of this
    structure are (a) sense predominates over meaning, (b) agglutination of
    semantic units, (c) the influx of "sense," and (d) it is idiomatic.[81]

Inner speech maintains its social origins and is "quasi-social;" however, it
remains distinct from external social speech. Vygotsky stated that "even if we
could record inner speech on a phonograph it would be condensed, fragmentary,
disconnected, unrecognizable, and incomprehensible in comparison to external
speech" (in Wertsch, 1985a, p. 173). It has been questioned as to why Vygotsky
did not use the term *inner dialogue* and it turns out that he did in some cases, yet
this was not his choice of terms for explaining the entire spectrum of inner speech.
At the same time Wertsch has suggested that the concepts *egocentric dialogue*
and *inner dialogue* would be more appropriate for a complete understanding of
Vygotsky's intentions. The very core of inner speech rests on the concept of
images, with the question then asked being, *Where do images come from?* The
answer cannot be given scientifically or statistically, and any discussion of the
emergence of forms or images will not fit into an algorithmic understanding of
psychology. It has been hypothesized by Russian psychologists that children
possess *miniature systems of knowledge*, which are primary *image models* (cf.
Stetsenko, 1989, p. 8). Davydov & Zinchenko (1981, p. 34) have stated that
images are subjective phenomena occurring as the result of practical, objective,
sensoriperceptual, and intellectual activity. An image is an integral reflection of
reality in which the basic perceptual categories are present all at the same time
(space, time, movement, color, form, number, etc.). In an attempt to separate
mind–body within Cartesian dualism, references to the *subconscious* are usually
deferred to Freud or are left out. Vygotsky's intense interest in aesthetics included
thoughts on the *unconscious/subconscious*, stating that

> The unconscious, it is said, is by definition something we do not recognize; it is some-
> thing unknown to us, and therefore it cannot become the subject of scientific investi-
> gation. This reasoning proceeds from the false assumption that we can study only what
> is directly recognizable. This is obviously a superficial approach, since we do study
> many things of which we have knowledge only from analogies, hypotheses, surmises,
> etc. (Vygotsky, 1971, p. 23)

He went on to say that even though geologists and historians do not know
more about the *subconscious/unconscious* than others, it does not stop them from
studying subjects that cannot be experienced. To give an example from current

---

[81]cf. Akutina (1987, pp. 14–15). Also see Vygotsky (1994a, p. 182). As well, refer to Wertsch (1985b,
p. 124), where he stated: "For the semantic characterization of inner speech he [Vygotsky] identified three interrelated properties: the predominance of 'sense' over 'meaning,' the tendency toward
'agglutination,' and the 'infusion of sense into a word.'" Also, refer to Vygotsky in *Thought and
Language* (1994a, pp. 84–86); and the last reference is Wertsch in Zivan (1979, pp. 79–85).

scholars, Noam Chomsky writes in a *scientific* fashion, yet he is most interested in the study of the *unconscious*. For example, Chomsky stated that ". . . I'm very much concerned with unconscious cognitive processes. It seems to me that the work we've done shows as conclusively as one can show with this kind of material that in these areas most of the processing of experience, at least with respect to language, is not only conscious but is beyond the range of conscious processes . . . As far as I have been able to determine, however, I'm not able to see anything in the Freudian tradition that tries to develop a notion of unconscious processes in the area of cognitive thinking. This seems to me a real gap" (Otero, 1988, pp. 123–124).

In returning to an understanding of inner speech two points need to be mentioned: (1) Within every sentence there is a "subtext," a term borrowed from Konstantin Stanislavsky, which was used in the theater. Actors were often given one simple line and were asked to interpret it up to 40 times or more in order to discover the *subtext*. Stanislavsky coined many neologisms within a rich texture of imagery, such as *superconscious* and *emotional memory*. (2) "Behind the plane of verbal thought there lies a level even more inward than inner speech: the plane of thought itself, and according to Vygotsky, 'the flow of thought is not accompanied by the simultaneous unfolding of speech'" (Bakhurst, 1986, p. 121). Although inner speech cannot ultimately be separated from external speech, its primary function serves as a controlling mechanism and its highest correlate is self-regulation. One possible route from internal to external speech is the following:

MOTIVE
      THOUGHT
            INNER SPEECH
                  SEMANTIC PLANNING
                      EXTERNAL SPEECH
                    (Akhutina, 1978, p. 18)

CONCEPT FORMATION

What follows are two initial lines of development from complex formation, through potential concepts to true concepts. Vygotsky placed value in *concept formation* regarding child development, such as Piaget's interest in establishing *operations*.

Two lines of thought need to be distinguished in understanding Vygotsky's and L. S. Sakharov's (Vygotsky's collaborator until 1928) research in concept formation: (1) Concepts are not formed by building associative chains, and (2)

Children do not possess mature concept formation, but go through an elaborate series of developments, using *protoconcepts* to finally reach a stage of abstract thinking. This approach is in direct opposition to behavorism and to the tenets of structural linguistics in general. Jerry Fodor (1972), who is diametrically opposed to the thoughts of Vygotsky, offers an example of structural-cognitive linguistic understanding on this subject:

> It is that if the conceptualizations of children are radically different from those of adults, it is extremely difficult to imagine how children and adults could ever manage to understand one another. All the more so if the alleged differences are supposed to be differences in word meanings, for that is to say that adults and children are, in a fairly strict sense, talking different languages; a situation only barely disguised by the similarities of the phonological and syntactic system the languages employ. Vygotsky's ways of dealing with this objection is simply hopeless. (p. 87)

Vygotsky addressed this problem in two ways 38 years after his death, offering an answer to the problem: Vygotsky claimed (1) "This method [which can be applied to Fodor] deals with the results of the completed process of concept formation, with the ready-made product of that process . . . Consequently, in studying definitions of developed concepts, we are frequently dealing less with the child's thinking than with his reproduction of fully formed knowledge and definitions" (Vygotsky, 1987, p. 121). (2) "The method of definition depends almost exclusively on the word. It overlooks the fact that, for the child in particular, the concept is linked with sensual material, the perception and transformation of which gives rise to the concept itself" (Vygotsky, 1987, p. 121). When setting up experiments, it was felt that concept formation should be studied by simultaneously introducing objects and words. Vygotsky's research in concept formation was in line with his entire philosophical framework of taking the highest possible stance as the guiding principle and measuring the results by that principle. His method of research was dialectical and historical in his terminology, meaning that change was measured over time. Research experiments were based on the understanding that the inner mental processes can be observed through experiments, all of which are designed to measure the development of the concept. Many (but not all) of the experiments were designed to test children individually, which has surprised many readers, thinking that Russian experiments would be conducted with groups. In reality, Vygotsky's approach was designed to gain information on the development of the unique individual, and his procedural method was also designed to better understand concept formation through the filter of functionalism.

When beginning experiments within their method of *dual stimulation*, Vygotsky and Sakharov based their experimental designs on a modified version of experiments of the German psychologist, Ach, who believed that concepts were not finished products. Vygotsky and Sakharov were convinced "that the method had to be developmental–synthetic, that is one should study the way words acquire significative meaning, the way they transform into symbols."[82] Since humans are not passive receivers of knowledge it is then understood that concepts serve a definite function; therefore, one must submit the subject of an experiment to conditions where concepts take on a functional role.

It should be pointed out that the understanding of goal formation was different from that of the proponents of Russian *activity theory*. For example, Vygotsky felt that although a goal must be in place to achieve growth and development, a process cannot be explained via a goal. Vygotsky said that

> . . . we cannot satisfactorily explain labor by saying that it is called to life by the goals and tasks with which man is faced. Labor must be explained in terms of the use of tools and the application of the means without which it could not arise. In precisely the same sense, the central problem for the explanation of the higher forms of behavior is the problem of the means through which man masters the processes of his own behavior. (Vygotsky, 1987, p. 126)

When setting up an experimental design the stimulus *sign* or *word* was used as the variable with the task being the constant. When conducting experiments it was understood that the "*development of the processes that eventually lead to the formation of concepts has its roots in the earliest stages of childhood. However, these processes mature only in the transitional age*" (Vygotsky, 1987, p. 130). With these thoughts in mind, Vygotsky and Sakharov developed a revised version of Ach's experiments by presenting the subjects with objects of different colors, shapes, weights, and heights. The names of the objects were written underneath them and there were nonsense words in Russian connected with the objects that took on new meanings, such as "bat" (small and low objects), "dek" (small and tall objects), and "mup" (large and tall objects). There were groups of 20 to 30 objects that were not organized that were all placed on a game board with an unequal number of objects in each category.

> The experimenter now turned one of the objects upside down, had the child read its name, and put it—with its name visible—in a separate segment of the board explaining that this was the toy of children from another culture and that there were more of these toys among the objects. It was explained that if the child would find the other "toys" he would win a prize. The child was encouraged to work carefully and slowly and the order in which he selected the "toys" was recorded as well as the time used. After the child had made an incorrect selection the experimenter would have him turn one of the objects not selected upside down and read its name . . . This new instance of the concept was then laid next to the first one and all other objects were put in their original place. The child, thus, had to start the selection process all over again, now having two instances of the concept at his disposal. This—rather frustrating—process continued until the child had correctly finished the task. In between the experimenter would ask the child to explain the reasons for his choice and to give a definition of the concept "toy." (van der Veer & Valsiner, 1991, p. 261)

[82]cf. van der Veer & Valsiner (1991, pp. 259–260).

These types of experiments were not only for children, because a similar idea was used with patients suffering from Parkinson's disease. For example, Vygotsky initially asked a patient to walk across the room alone, often resulting in tremors. However, when pieces of paper were placed across the floor touching each other, the patient could understand the dual stimulation intuitively and could take steps going from paper to paper, often with the tremors stopping (cf. Wertsch, 1991, p. 32). If one were to visit many hospital settings today a similar concept would be experienced, initially using the same model of laying out papers, which has now been expanded to virtual reality visors patients wear in order to walk; patients can use visors instead of having the pieces of paper laid out so that they can walk outside.

Vygotsky implemented a *functional method of dual or double stimulation* in all of his experiments of this type.

> We regard the functional method of two-fold stimulation . . . as most adequate to our task. Seeking to study the inner structure of the higher psychological processes, we do not limit ourselves to the usual method of offering the subject simple stimuli . . . to which we expect a direct response; we simultaneously offer a second series of stimuli which must play a functionally special role, serving as a means by which the subject can organize his own behaviour. In this way we study the *process of accomplishing a task by the aid of certain auxiliary means,* and the whole psychological structure of the act thus proves to be within our reach over the entire course of its development and in all the variety of each of its phases. (Vygotsky & Luria, 1994, p. 159)

Vygotsky wanted to demonstrate that what lay behind the meaning of the child's word was a three dimensional, not a one-dimensional space. He also wanted to show that concepts "are nothing other than processed perceptions and ideas. In a word, thinking is preceded by sensations, perceptions, ideas, etc. not the reverse" (Vygotsky, 1989, p. 67). In using the method of double stimulation no time frame was given and usually the beginning of the experiment or warm-up time was disqualified in writing up the results.

What follows are two lines of development from complex formation, through concepts to true concepts. Vygotsky was not so much concerned with establishing stages of development that corresponded to exact ages of children but was more interested in the functional role of speech in the formation of concepts.[83] With that thought in mind, the stages of concept formation are as follows:

1. *Syncretism,* which simply means placing unorganized heaps together, which was referred to by Blonsky as the *incoherent coherence* (sometimes translated as the *unconnected connectedness*).[84] There are three subcomponents

[83]cf. El'konin [Elkonin] (1967, p. 36).
[84]The term *unconnected connectedness* is translated in Rieber (1987, p. 136).

to this phase which include (a) trial-and-error, "selecting arbitrary objects and trying arbitrary others when corrected" (van der Veer & Valsiner, 1991, p. 263), (b) children selecting objects spatially close to each other in the original formation, and (c) a vague category, yet "one gets the impression that in this the children selected various syncretic groups, from which they selected several objects to form yet another syncretic group" (van der Veer & Valsiner, 1991, p. 263).

2. *Complexes*: During this stage children start to arrange objects on the basis of some concrete objective feature or criterion, which is not always apparent to adults. Some subgroups will share certain properties with complexes being broken down into (a) *associative complexes*, where the child adds on to objects by virtue of similar features. Vygotsky stated that at this stage "words stop being proper names and become family names,"[85] (b) *collections*, "where objects are now grouped together according to features which are complementary to each other." Thus when the starting object is a yellow pyramid the child will add objects with other colors and another form until all forms and colors are represented,"[86] (c) *chain complexes*, where if a child starts off with a green circle, then he or she adds other circles found. If the last circle is red, then perhaps all red objects will be placed together, (d) *diffuse complexes*, where a clear understanding of the relationships remains diffuse; for example, a child might start with a yellow triangle, then add a trapezium because the form is similar (cf. van der Veer & Valsiner, 1991, p. 264).

3. *Pseudoconcepts*. "A pseudo-concept is the transitional construct between complexes and concepts. It is transitional because the relationship between sign and non-linguistic reality is similar to that in genuine concepts, but the relationship between sign and other signs is difference" (Wertsch, 1985b, p. 105). Pseudo-concepts[87] function as a bridge between child and adult understanding and without them there would be little meaningful communication. At the same time, the usage of pseudoconcepts is common among adults,

---

[85]Sakharov is being quoted at this point. See van der Veer & Valsiner (1991, p. 264).

[86]Ibid., p. 264.

[87]For a good discussion on pseudo-concepts in German, with Russian examples, see Rissom (1985, pp. 278–285). For example: "Die Entstehung von Pseudobegriffen hat ihre Wurzeln im "obšcenie", im sprachlichen Verkehr zwischen Erwachsenem und Kind . . . ; anders herum betrachtet, erweist sich das Auftreten von Pseudobegriffen gleichzeitig als von besonderer funktionaler Bedeutung für den Verkehr . . . Die wesentliche Funktion von Pseudobegriffen sieht Vygotskij [Vygotsky] darin, daß Kind und Erwachsener sich trotz unterschiedlicher Denkweisen verständigen können" (p. 281). Translation: "The origin of pseudo-concepts has its roots in 'obšcenie,' in linguistic interaction between the adult and the child; viewing it in a different way, the appearance of pseudo-concepts proves to be simultaneous within a special functional meaning for the linguistic interaction . . . Vygotsky sees the essential function of pseudo-concepts in the fact that the child and the adult can make themselves understood (i.e., can understand each other), despite varying thought processes." [DR]

particularly in ritualized–*phatic* communication. "The adult constantly shifts from conceptual to concrete, complex thinking. The transitional, pseudoconceptual form of thought is not confined to the child's thinking; we too resort to it very often in our daily lives" (Vygotsky, 1994a, p. 134). In general, one can say that the patterns and products used in pseudoconcepts resemble those used in real concepts; however, the environment primarily influences the reasoning involved at the pseudoconceptual level.

> It is precisely when children are capable of operating with decontextualized word meanings alone without being distracted by the nonlinguistic context that one can speak of the movement from thinking in complexes and pseudoconcepts to thinking in genuine, especially scientific concepts. (Wertsch, 1985b, pp. 106–107)

Once a child starts to use correct names in relatively decontextualized situations, it is wrong to assume that they mean the same thing as adults do. The bridge between children's pseudoconcepts and adults' real concepts has been called *functional equivalents* by a contemporary of Vygotsky, Dmitr Uznadze.

> Words take over the function of concepts and may serve as means of communication long before they reach the level of concepts characteristic of fully developed thought ... Uznadze suggested that a special study should be undertaken of what he called "functional equivalents" of concepts. The methodological difficulty in designing such a study stems from the fact that, as their name suggests, the child's preconceptual representations are often functionally equivalent to concepts. The functional aspect, therefore, cannot serve as a basis for discrimination between preconceptual and conceptual forms of thinking. (Kozulin, 1990, p. 158)

Although pseudoconcepts look like real concepts, when children, learners, or participants in experiments are asked to define them, it then becomes evident that the child or initiate does not have a full grasp of the meaning of the particular concept. For example, during an experiment it was noted that children would often speak words of astonishing complexity, but when visitors stopped by (i.e., researchers would use such occasions to stop the experiment in order to ask the children for definitions), the children were not able to respond. Often the responses were surprising to those who had heard the child or who had learned to use the concept appropriately many times. This lesson has profound ramifications for second language acquisition;[88] indeed Vygotsky used this idea when speaking about the learning of a second language.[89] The last comments are taken from Kozulin (1990) who focused on the aspect of *action* to *thought*, when he said that "the operation of pseudoconceptual thought suggest that the principle

---

[88]"Children who do not possess the appropriate generalization are often unable to communicate their experience. The problem is not the lack of the appropriate words or sounds, but the absence of the appropriate concept or generalization. Without the latter, understanding is impossible" (Vygotsky, 1987, p. 49).

[89]See Kozulin (1990, p. 163).

'from action to thought' should be applied not only to the development of intelligence, but also to its functioning" (p. 163). When describing the development of concepts, it is clear that action precedes thought in the initial stages. Vygotsky spoke about very young children who first paint a picture and then describe it. The reverse process comes later, and indeed there are many true concepts that will never be totally defined, yet they are understood. In focusing on *thought*, there is at the same time a realization that many thought processes emerge from the unconscious, often via images that are perhaps tied to archetypes not understood in the conscious mind. The interest in preserving the aspect of *thought*, as opposed to concentrating on *action or activity*, will lead to self-regulated action.

4.   *Potential concepts*: Following Groos, Vygotsky maintained that potential concepts can be viewed as a product of habit and are not only capable of realization in humans. "Potential concepts result from a series of isolating abstractions of such a primitive nature that they are present to some degree in very young children but even in animals" (Vygotsky, 1994a, p. 137). Even the first words of children resemble potential concepts, which are then preintellectual; therefore, potential concepts can be found both in perceptual thinking and in "practical, action-bound thinking."[90] The inclusion of the potential concept is an excellent example of Vygotsky's genetic–developmental thinking. What differentiates the various complexes and concepts is the representation of varying functional needs.

5.   *True concepts*: At this point decontextualization takes place, which is usually viewed as a sign of maturing. It should be mentioned that Vygotsky was of the opinion that visual thinking breaks off with the formation of concepts, turning to fantasy in the adolescent. "It is for this reason . . . that, during the early stages of puberty, the spontaneous visual images often appear even when the arbitrarily evoked images have completely ceased to happen" (van der Veer & Valsiner, 1994, p. 273). Vygotsky stated that E. R. Jaensch's conception of *eidetic images* (e.g., often referring to "afterimages") dominated primitive stages of human culture, both in the ontogenetic and phylogenetic periods, yet with cultural development these eidetic images are subsumed into abstract thinking. The focus within this context is on *thought* more than *action*, although these two aspects form a contiguous whole. E. R. Jaensch had a tremendous influence upon Vygotsky, defining *eidetic imagery* as such:

> Optical perceptual (or eidetic) images are phenomena that take up an intermediate position between sensations and images . . . they are always *seen* in the literal sense. They have this property of necessity under all conditions, and share it with sensations . . . For the great majority of adults there is an unbridgeable gulf between sensations and images . . . Because of the fluctuations in the personality . . . We cannot assign one definite point to the eidetic image, but must assign to it a finite range within

[90]Vygotsky (1994a, p. 138).

which the phenomenon can fluctuate according to the momentarily operative
functional circumstances . . . now approaching one pole, now the other. (Jaensch, 1930,
pp. 1–3)

The discussion of images is important at this point, because it is hypothesized that adults function within a conceptual framework, which is in need of the
inclusion of the *general genetic law of images*, paralleling the same law for development. In other words, images often remain at the external level of social origins,
without being mediated as a regulatory principle, or they are quickly absorbed
and stored at the unconscious level. Sergei Eisenstein (a famous Russian film pro-
ducer and semiotician) not only influenced the European cinema (in particular
German films during the 1920s and 1930s, especially Fritz Lang) but also influenced Vygotsky as well. Vygotsky's cousin, David, was a recognized linguist in
Moscow and he is attributed with establishing a study circle on semiotics, including Marr, Eisenstein, Vygotsky, and others attending. This circle was active during
1928, which was a most productive year for Vygotsky's writings. Eisenstein maintained that

thought processes must be viewed as simultaneously "thematic-logical" and "image-
sensual," with the latter clearly in a dominant role . . . In "image-sensual" structure, a
prelogical syncretic form of thinking, a concept is conveyed not by an abstract gener-
alizing sign, but by members of paradigm classes bearing either metonmymic or
metaphorical relationship to aspects of the complex concept. (Eagle in Bailey et al.,
1980, pp. 174–175)

The theme of image is to be related holistically within the entire range of
Vygotsky's thinking. From here the history of concept formation continues in an
analysis of scientific (educational) and spontaneous (everyday) concepts.[91]

SCIENTIFIC AND SPONTANEOUS CONCEPTS

The word scientific in Russian (i.e., *nauchnii*) can be expanded in translation to also include *academic* or *scholarly*.[92] Scientific concepts[93] refer to a school

---

[91]Although no mention of social interaction has been given relating to concept formation, there is an
interesting connection. G. H. Mead has been compared to Vygotsky by many scholars, beginning
with Jerome Bruner. Mead contributed to interesting ideas along the lines of action, the social
element, images, and so forth. However, Mead, as a social interactionist, was not an experimenter,
did not conceive of his theories along a genetic–developmental line, and did not have the same
understanding of history as change. One interesting article on the comparison of Mead and
Vygotsky is by lbolya Vari-Szilagyi (1991) titled: "G. H. Mead and L. S. Vygotsky on Action."
Studies in Soviet Thought, Vol. 42, pp. 93–121.

[92]For a closer examination of the term *nauchnii*, refer to Wertsch (1992, p. 123).

[93]"According to Vygotsky, scientific concepts differ from pseudoconcepts primarily in that (1) they
are determined by other concepts, and are part of a conceptual system; (2) they are cognized as

setting, whereas spontaneous concepts refer to learning in everyday life. In order to progress along the continuum of concept development both of these aspects need to function together dialectically. The scientific concept is viewed within a "top-down" approach, with the spontaneous concept being experienced in a "bottom-up" fashion. Within the school setting a concrete bridge joining these two concepts together in a holistic fashion can be found in the application and learning of grammar, according to Vygotsky. It is at this point that grammar is understood before logic; in other words, children use grammar on a day-to-day basis, often without being able to analyze it; yet once they receive instruction in grammar, there is a process of objectification in the child's mind. In differentiating between scientific and spontaneous concepts, the former maintains systematicity, whereas the latter is placed within a different system, which should not be labeled as being *nonsystematic.*

> Scientific concepts, with their hierarchical system of interrelation, seem to be the medium within which awareness and mastery first develop, to be transferred later to other concepts and other areas of thought. Reflective consciousness comes to the child through the portals of scientific concepts. (Vygotsky, 1994a, p. 171)

This statement might be surprising and what is meant is that in the everyday world of reality, young children's experiences are mostly lived out, not constantly reflected on for further action. For example, Vygotsky gave the example of young children painting a picture and describing what the picture meant to them. Only later do children learn to think of an idea and describe that idea, before painting it.[94] Both spontaneous and scientific concepts are not stable units of understanding, and both maintain a multidirectional *flow* within a dialectical continuum.

> Scientific concepts do not emerge smoothly and directly from spontaneous concepts. Rather, the two types of concepts follow different courses and play different roles in theory development . . . There is a dialectic interaction between spontaneous and scientific concepts. As a result of this interaction, "true concepts" emerge. (Au, 1992, p. 272)

It is also accepted that everyday concepts mediate scientific concepts and in reality they are different ends of one continuum, although they have evolved

concepts, i.e., a concept is cognized separately from its denotata; (3) 'supraempirical' connections, i.e., connections that take place only between concepts, but not between their denotata, are possible in such cases. These characteristics are associated with the use of scientific concepts in a specific sphere of activity: science. Everyday concepts used in 'everyday life' (which for Vygotsky means 'not in science') do not need to be defined and cognized separately from their denotata" (Tul'viste, 1989b, pp. 6–7).

[94] "Children who do not posses the appropriate generalization are often unable to communicate their experience. The problem is not the lack of the appropriate words or sounds, but the absence of the appropriate concept or generalization. Without the latter, understanding is impossible" (Vygotsky, 1987, p. 49).

under varying conditions. Vygotsky spoke directly about the relationship of these two concepts within the learning of a foreign language:

> It is well known that to learn a foreign language at school and to develop one's native language involve two entirely different processes. While learning a foreign language, we use word meanings that are already well developed in the native language, and only translate them; the advanced knowledge of one's own language also plays an important role in the study of the foreign one, as well as those inner and outer relations that are characteristic only in the study of a foreign language. And yet in spite of all these differences, the acquisition of the foreign and native languages belongs to one general class of the processes of speech development. (Vygotsky, 1994a, p. 159)

A similar statement is reflected by Sasha Felix in foreign language learning, stating that "if cognition were the major determining factor in L1 and L2, acquisition would be totally dissimilar as a result of the learner's different cognitive status" (Felix, 1981, p. 180).

Vygotsky wrote about the heuristic value of learning scientific concepts that ultimately reaches beyond the immediate experience of the child. In the example of the foreign language, the semantics of L1 are used as a safety net for a long time when practicing L2. However,

> the development of concepts, both spontaneous and scientific, belongs to the semantic aspect of speech development; from the psychological point of view, the development of concepts and the development of words meanings are but two forms of one and the same process, which imprints its characteristic signature on both. (Vygotsky, 1994a, p. 160)

It should be mentioned that Vygotsky's understanding of scientific concepts changed during the last ten years of his life. He went from focusing on the psychological and semiotic nature of scientific concept forms to discourse used primarily in formal schooling" (Wertsch & Minick, 1990, p. 83). If Vygotsky had lived longer, his understanding of the *scientific concept* would have probably been extended.

SUMMARY OF THOUGHT, WORD MEANING, LANGUAGE, AND CONCEPT FORMATION

It is at this point that a synthesis and review is given: Vygotsky considered *thought* and *speech* to be the key to understanding the nature of human consciousness, yet speech does not create higher psychological processes—it transforms them.[95] *Thought* and *speech* are said to have different genetic roots, with

---

[95]See B. Bain (Ed.) (1983, p. 25).

a prelinguistic stage in *thought*, and a pre-intellectual stage in *speech*, although many Soviet scholars have not accepted this position. These two stages follow different developmental lines, meeting somewhere around the age of two, where functional needs change, with the *word* taking on the same function as problem solving in activity. In the beginning of life the child does not understand the concepts around him or her, with gestures serving the role of *"object regulation"* (e.g., pointing to objects). The meaning that results is supplied externally by the parents or caregivers. Once the child realizes that a reaction can be obtained by gesturing, intentions are formed and the child learns to point with intention, hence *"other regulation."* Once internalization takes place, inner speech (which is a separate function from external speech) allows for *"self-regulation."* The stages of internalization are as follows: preintellectual, egocentric speech,[96] naive psychology, which includes the ingrowth stage, also called *rooting*,[97] or *ingrowth*. This is a *seamlike ingrowing*, where the "... seam connecting to parts of organic texture very rapidly leads to the formation of the connecting texture, so that the seam itself becomes unnecessary" (van der Veer & Valsiner, 1994, p. 66). Once internalization (sometimes referred to as *appropriation* or *mastery*)[98] takes place, inner speech (which is a separate function from external speech) allows for *"self-regulation."* At this point there is a continual, multidirectional dialectic between *word–thought–word*, and after a long period of time the interpsychological becomes internalized within the intrapsychological. In returning to the line of development of *speech* and *thought*, the unit of analysis of *word meaning* is used to comprehend dialectical, internal relationships in order to better understand consciousness and the higher mental processes. The reason Vygotsky selected *word meaning* as his basic *unit of analysis* of consciousness was to establish a procedure that could be used to analyze the smallest components of a unit, all of which maintain the essence of the whole. The example of H_2O was given. With this example, Vygotsky attempted to isolate the internal side of

---

[96]Thoughts on Piaget are left out because of the expanded nature of the discourse. Much of Vygotsky's thoughts on *inner speech* were derived from criticisms based on Piaget's *egocentric speech*.

[97]See Emerson (1983, p. 253).

[98]Barbara Rogoff (Wertsch et al., 1995, p. 152) wrote: "Some scholars use the term 'internalization' in ways resembling how I use the term 'participatory appropriation.' Translations of Vygotsky often refer to internalization, but his concept may be similar to my notion of appropriation . . . I first noticed the word 'appropriation' in Balchtin's (1981) writing, as I was searching for a way to express the difference between my views and the version of internalization involving importing objects across boundaries from external to internal. Bakhtin argued that the words people use belong partially to others, as they appropriate words from others and adapt them to their own purposes." Another example regards A. N. Leontiev, who referred to Piaget. ". . . Leont'ev [Leontiev] replaces Piaget's concept of 'assimilation' with the concept of 'appropriation.' With this distinction he moves from a biologically oriented metaphor to a socio-historical one" (Newman et al., 1989, p. 62).

word meaning in order to juxtapose it dialectically with the external side of *word*, which ultimately results in an asymmetrical unity. *Word meaning* is then broken down into *sense* and *meaning*, implying that sense is the personal, fluid interpretation that can change according to contexts, whereas meaning is more stable. The example was given of words found in a dictionary for specific, stabilized meaning. For Vygotsky every word was at the same time a generalization (e.g., generalization = exclusion from visual structures and the inclusion in thought structures and in semantic structures),[99] which implies that the word is not only present in language, but in thought as well. Thought is then generated by motive, not by thought, and for understanding to take place the connecting points must be meaningful. In viewing the stages of concepts, the child experiences many lines of regrouping in order to develop and reach the level of *pseudoconcept*, where it appears that real concepts are being used, until the child–adolescent is asked for a specific definition of the word or concept being implemented. Then it is apparent that the adult and the child or sometimes the adolescent have varying degrees of understanding of one word, or different understandings of the same concept. It has also been stated that adults use *pseudoconcepts* in everyday speech, where normal misunderstandings arise because of the instability of these *pseudoconcepts*. V. Zinchenko refers to this zone of normal miscommunication as the *delta position*.[100] One of the points being made here is the focus on *thought* related to *action*, realizing that both form a dialectical whole.

> The operation of pseudoconceptual thought suggests that the principle "from action to thought" should be applied not only to the development of intelligence, but also to its function . . . This double-faceted nature of thought suggests that the interpretative or metacognitive function of consciousness may have a certain autonomy from regulative and controlling functions. In simple terms, it means that there is a great difference between an intelligent-looking action, and an adequate knowledge of one's own intellectual operations. (Kozulin, 1990, p. 163)

What is meant is that often young children take action and then meaning is ascribed to the action, and indeed, this can take place with adults as well. The purpose of focusing on *thought* within the postmodern context, where action is a given, does not imply that real concepts or adult concepts are premeditated or always constructed beforehand; nor will human consciousness probably ever reach the level of being able to derive a complete understanding of adult thought processes. Certainly much of this model originates in the subconscious, being mediated by images. In finishing the summary, there is a view to *spontaneous* and *scientific* concepts, and it is safe to say that Vygotsky's interpretation would be different if he had lived longer. Today, "more and more, psychologists agree

[99]Vygotsky (1997, p. 138).
[100]Personal interview in Moscow on May 15, 1999.

that the thought of an educated person can by no means be wholly identified with certain characteristic operations of scientific thought" (Tul'viste [Tulviste], 1989b, p. 11); and even concept formation has been criticized as being "an artificial method that was not adequate for studying concepts because correct use of many concepts does not require their definition" (Tul'viste [Tulviste], 1989, p. 7).

Even though much criticism has been given to Vygotsky's theory of concept formation,[101] readers do not need to look beyond Vygotsky himself for a critical self-appraisal of his thoughts. In this regard Lev Semyonovich stated directly, "An experimentally evoked process of concept formation never reflects in mirror form the real genetic process of development as it occurs in reality" (Vygotsky quoted in El'konin, 1967, p. 36). Even with the many criticisms offered regarding Vygotsky's theories of concept formation, it is remarkable how current and popular they remain in so many fields.

DIALECTICS

Vygotsky's understanding of dialectics can be traced to his youth where he was involved in study circles that included discussions of Hegel. A childhood friend of Lev Semonovich, Semyon Dobkin remembers that

> Inspite of his age, Lev managed to bring some extraordinary elements, worth remembering in more detail, to our studies. To begin with, I must say that he had little interest in the pragmatic study of history . . . We wanted to find answers to such questions as "What is history?," "What distinguishes one people from another?," "What is the role of the individual in history?" In other words, we studied the philosophy of history. Vygotsky was at the time very enthusiastic about the Hegelian formula "thesis, antithesis, synthesis," and he applied it to analyzing historical events. (Dobkin, 1982, p. 26)

Vygotsky's conception of the dialectic was more in line with classical Marxist philosophy, using the dialectic primarily as a heuristic in order to impute a *dynamic* sense of change into his theoretical framework. Much of Vygotsky's works are based on dialectical principles and it is important to realize that the dialectic is not a scientific, inductive approach used to arrive at a finished product (i.e., ergon). Indeed Engels stated that there are no hard and fast rules in dialectics (cf. Engels, 1925, p. 153). There is a difference in the understanding of the

---

[101]"As happened so often in his work, he did not present the raw material in the form of protocols and he never gave an example of a classification based on a pseudoconcept versus a classification based on a real concept. It is, consequently, rather difficult to understand the difference between pseudoconcepts and real concepts. One gets the impression that what Sakharov and Vygotsky had in mind were, respectively, a classification based on perceptually given features versus a classification based on geometrical properties possible explicitly stated in the form of a definition" (van der Veer & Valsiner, 1991, p. 267).

dialectic for Hegel and for Engels, with the former viewing consciousness itself as being dialectic. For Engels, however, ". . . consciousness reflected the external dialectic of nature and history" (Levine, 1984, p. 83). The dialectic contains no exact element where proof can be obtained and it possesses only a small element of deduction. The word dialectic (Greek: dialégesthai) has the literal meaning of *conversation*, and it is often forgotten that the *dialectic proceeds not according to a contradictory but according to a contrary opposition.*[102] In operationalizing the dialectic two differing values must be attributed to it, one being the *conceptual dialectic*, which is more ideal, atemporal, and is found in purely logical relations. The other aspect, the *empirical dialectic*, relates to the real world, describing processes that take place in time and space.[103] In reality, one needs to divide the dialectic into its ideal and practical realms, being aware of which aspect is being discussed. This is especially true when relating the dialectic to the scientific realm, for the simple reason that

> scientific research can in fact be unaware of its own principal features. Dialectical knowledge, in contrast, is knowledge of the dialectic. For science, there is not any formal structure, nor any implicit assertion about the rationality of the universe: Reason *is developing*, and the mind prejudges nothing. In complete contrast, the dialectic is both a method *and* a movement in the object. (Sartre, 1976, p. 20)

In using the *dialectic*, Vygotsky transcended the "mind/body" problem in various respects; for example: "the Vygotskian approach . . . shatters this dualism and emphasizes the development of the individual in social interaction; specifically, the individual is formed through the internalization of activities carried out in . . . society" (Rosa & Montero, 1992, p. 83). However, the problem still exists regarding the unity or disunity of *individual mental functioning* and *cultural, institutional, and historical processes*. James Wertsch gave a hopeful solution to this problem from his sociocultural perspective on mediated action, stating that

> From this perspective my claim is that "mental functioning" and "sociocultural setting" are to be understood as terms referring to dialectically interacting moments, or aspects of *human action*. In this view human action is not to be interpreted solely on the basis of factors having to do with individuals or society in isolation, although part of my argument is that there are individual and societal moments to any action. In contrast to reductionistic approaches, human action is viewed here as providing a context within which individual and society (. . . mental functioning and sociocultural setting) are understood as interrelated moments. (Wertsch, 1995b, p. 88)

Vygotsky's concept of *social consciousness* is the point where biological mechanisms begin to recede in the background and where "socially constructed

[102]cf. Brugger (1972, pp. 93–94).
[103]cf. Norman & Sayers (1980, p. 67).

psychological activity *mediates* the impact of internal and external stimuli . . ." (Ratner, 1991, p. 3). Within this system of dialectics the individual does not experience social relations as something completely external, and although the individual as a particular derives consciousness, that aspect remains a generalization or idealization of experience.

DIALECTICS AND SPINOZA

Within the *dialectic* Vygotsky placed emphasis on *synthesis* more so than on *thesis* or *antithesis*. *Synthesis* is not to be positioned within openness, which would contradict Vygotsky's belief in Spinoza. This principle is sometimes called *dialectical monism* (Jean-Paul Sartre), and can be generally defined in the following way, although it does not directly relate to Vygotsky, and is not totally in line with Spinozian monism:

> Hence, the notion of totality does not imply that dialectical reasoning attempts to overcome a dualistic ontological position through a monistic reduction . . . Reduction also implies the substitution of dualistic notions by monistic ones. But dialectical thinking is not monistic. Dialectical reasoning attempts to transcend dualism as well as monism, by operating with a "unified" framework, one that presupposes the category of totality. (Israel, 1979, pp. 60–61)

Two points of clarification are necessary at this stage. Spinoza began by distinguishing between two types of affections: (a) *actions*, "which are explained by the nature of the affected individual, and which spring from the individual's essence" (Deleuze, 1981, p. 27), and (b) *passions*, "which are explained by something else, and which originate outside the individual" (Deleuze, 1981, p. 27). Therefore

> he [Spinoza] believed that human freedom was not, as was commonly held, indeterminacy of choice, but was self-determination, entirely by one's own nature, free from external compulsion. This, for him, was action proper, while determination by extraneous causes was passion, the subjection to which he called bondage. (Harris, 1992, p. 6)

At the same time, Spinoza "did not accept the existence of Descartes' free, undetermined soul and refuted his dualism. This attitude was very important to Vygotsky, whose aims were similar . . ." (van der Veer & Valsiner, 1991, p. 356). Together these ideas formed a part of the personal ethic by which Vygotsky lived and that he practiced in very difficult personal times.[104] Vygotsky was surely

---

[104]There was a major difference of opinion between A. N. Leontiev and Vygotsky in the early 1930s, and the following is taken from a letter from by Vygotsky to Leontiev in August 1933: "I feel

interested in Spinoza for many reasons, in particular the monistic solution of the body–soul problem.[105] Vygotsky has been criticized for being confusing in the sense that he firmly believed in Spinoza, who did not incorporate the usual understanding of *dialectic* into his philosophy. However, this confusion arises from a conflation of different ontological levels, with Vygotsky being a Spinozian at the highest levels of understanding, and a philosophical Marxist at the level of societal and individual consciousness. As well, the concept of *determinism* needs to be redefined. For example:

> Since Spinoza was an eminent determinist, it followed from Vygotsky's presentation that a new form of determinism was generated in the philosophy of Spinoza-as a methodological base of a new psychological theory free of the birthmarks of the Cartesian method of thinking. According to Vygotsky, this theory has as its subject man as an integral and active psychophysical being, striving toward self-development, motivated only by bodily–spiritual needs. Its key category is the concept of motivation. (Yaroshevsky, 1999, p. 264)

PROBLEMS REGARDING VYGOTSKY'S UNDERSTANDING OF DIALECTICS

Vygotsky's dialectics have been questioned on many accounts, but two points of relevance are mentioned:

(1) The first point revolves around the connection of the dialectic and education. Within the Zone of Proximal Development it appears that there is only a unidirectional movement toward the highest level of the higher mental processes, hence no sense of asymmetrical dialectic. In general, relating to the field of education it can be stated that this criticism is true within the Zone of Proximal Development. Indeed, learners do not continually progress toward a higher level of development and understanding, and in all human life there is not only progression but also a certain type of *regression*. This aspect was indirectly addressed by Vygotsky when he discussed the fact that development in education is not linear but *spiral* (cf. van der Veer & Valsiner, 1991, p. 309); however, this does not account for regression as a normal factor in development. For example:

> If Vygotsky emphasized the dialectical restructuring of organisms in the progressive phase of development, then a similar qualitatively new restructuring should be accepted to be in place at the regressive phases of the process. . . . if Vygotsky's idea

already and not for the first time that we stand before a very important conversation, as it were, for which we both, apparently, are not prepared, and the contents of which we can only vaguely imagine—your departure [for Kharkov]—is our serious, maybe irremediable, failure, resulting from our errors and real negligence of the cause that has been entrusted to us. Apparently, neither in your biography, nor in mine, nor in the history of our psychology, will what has happened be repeated. So be it. I am trying to understand all this in the Spinozist way—with sadness but accepting it as something inevitable" (van der Veer & Valsiner, 1991, p. 290).

[105]See van der Veer & Valsiner (1991, p. 356).

> of developmental dialectical synthesis is followed with rigor it is not possible for any organism to regress to a *previous* stage/state of development. Instead, the organism may become transformed from a higher to a lower state or stage, but that would *not* constitute retracing of a previously traversed path in development. Vygotsky did not express himself clearly in this matter . . . (van der Veer & Valsiner, 1991, p. 176)

Indeed, Vygotsky spoke to the fact that *culture* and *sign systems* must be passed down to future generations, yet his focus was on the method of the Socratic dialogue, which he had experienced himself with his private tutor of many years, Solomon Aspiz. As a teacher Aspiz was a firm believer in role modeling the highest cultural and educational theories possible, yet the discussions with Vygotsky were of a give-and-take nature of Socratic negotiation.

It should be stated that Vygotsky was of the opinion that

> dynamic psychology has a double task: to distinguish the lower forms imbedded in the higher, but also to reveal how the higher forms mature out of the lower ones. This double task could be accomplished only if one accepts that not only the individual him- or herself, but each one of the psychological formations . . . could become a subject of developmental analysis. (Kozulin, 1990, p. 213)[106]

Indeed, it should be remembered that Vygotsky's understanding of the Zone of Proximal Development took place during the last two years of his life when he was very ill. Although Vygotsky did not write about regression in general he spent time researching and working with mentally retarded children, outlining theoretical concepts that would allow them to live up to their highest potential.

(2) A second argument revolves around Vygotsky's lack of dialectical understanding regarding the juxtaposition of the individual and the environment within the dialectic. It is sometimes stated that Vygotsky did not regard the influence of the environment on the individual, and from the point of view of contemporary understanding of the environment this is certainly true. However regarding the educational setting Vygotsky stated that his focus was intentionally directed toward the learner and not toward the influence that the environment has on the learner. This approach parallels Vygotsky's analysis of art by focusing on the subject matter and not on the expanded periphery. However, in other contexts, Vygotsky directly addressed the role of the environment by stating that "the dialectical approach, while admitting the influence of nature on man, asserts that man, in turn affects nature and creates through his changes in nature new natural conditions for his existence" (Vygotsky, 1978, p. 60). Vygotsky did write about an example of the structured environment relating to a single mother and her three children. It is then concluded by van der Veer & Valsiner (1991) that

> For Vygotsky, the relevance of the interaction with the structured environment was the utilization of the latter as the *resource* for the child's psychic life-experiences and

---

[106]For a more detailed discussion on regression, see van der Veer & Valsiner (1991, pp. 210–225). Also see Tharp & Gallimore (1988, pp. 38–43).

meanings, that were seen as the intricate link that connected the developing child and the environment into a mutual relation . . . It is the child's experiencing (*perezhivanie*) of the environment, organized by the use of meanings (the socially constructed "stimulus-means") that constitute the essence of the study of environment for Vygotsky's system of paedology. (p. 316)[107]

In closing the discussion on dialectics it should *not* be assumed that Vygotsky accepted all of the tenets of Spinoza uncritically. For example, there is some evidence to show that Vygotsky perhaps became convinced "that no simple answers for the problem of dualism in psychology were to be found in Spinoza's writings" (van der Veer & Valsiner, 1991, p. 357). It is however argued that Vygotsky understood that the genetic–developmental progression of personality took place within the context of dialectics, positioned or anchored within Spinoza's monism. It is also argued that this position was coherent in all of his writings from the beginning until the end of his career. The next section views Vygotsky's approach to aesthetics, which remained the underlying focus of his later thoughts in psychology.

AESTHETICS

This summary differs from the previous ones and is offered as an introduction to the aesthetic theories that accompanied Vygotsky most of his life. It has been hypothesized that his interest in psychology resulted in part from a desire to better understand aesthetics; as well, it has been suggested that although Vygotsky did not publish any books on aesthetics from 1925 onward, that was due to the political climate of the country. In beginning this section the core of aesthetics for Vygotsky was *inner speech* and the heart of inner speech is the *image*. It is clear from this description that Vygotsky assigned an aesthetic meaning to the subconscious.

> Any conscious and reasonable interpretation or comment given to a work of art by the artist or the reader must be regarded as a subsequent rationalization, as a self-deception, a justification before one's own intellect, or an explanation devised post factum. (Vygotsky, 1971, p. 72)

With this positioning on the side of the subconscious, Vygotsky then described the necessary aspects of emotion, written in contradistinction to the Russian formalist school. This school of thought transcended the emotional functions of art by using art in a political way to free the *material* of its tradi-

---

[107]Peadology or pedology was a term that fused concepts such as child psychology, educational psychology, and child experimental psychology. Vygotsky actively supported efforts in pedology by lecturing at the Herzen University in St. Petersburg, writing scholarly words, and conducting child experiments in psychology. This direction in education was finally banned in 1936 in Russia, and was a major excuse for condemning the works of Vygotsky.

tional *form*. For Vygotsky the *effect* generated in art is exactly what distinguishes art from other areas, such as science. Vygotsky's understanding of *emotions* was based on his acceptance of Spinozian philosophy, differentiating two forms of affections: *actions* and *passions*. Actions are the result of self-regulation involving the individual power of acting on; passions, on the other hand, are described as originating from outside the individual, where a person is acted on. It was during his youth that Vygotsky studied not only Spinoza, but also areas such as *the active form of the word, word and image, verbal representation of consciousness*, and so on, ideas that were later used in relating to his scientific inquires. It has already been stated that Vygotsky was most influenced by a Ukrainian linguist, A. A. Potebnya, who began his linguistic analysis with the study of the *word*. Potebnya stated that the role of the word is not the same for the speaker as it is for the listener. The inner form of a word is an image unrelated to the word, but is its "essential." Potebnya went on to specify that all significations are *imagistic* in origin and images are more familiar to us than that which they explain, concluding that the poetic image is always an allegory. Potebnya specified what he meant in terms of allegory by distinguishing between *synecdoche* ("in which what is designated by an image is a part of the signification, or vice versa"), and *metonymy* ("in which an image, as it were, renames what it designates on the basis of a contiguity of significations").[108] Sergei Eisenstein also referred to similar properties within the cinematic language of "image–sensual" structures and "thematic–logical" structures, with the former playing a dominant role. Eisenstein stated that

> in "image–sensual" structure . . . a concept is conveyed not by an abstract generalizing sign, but by members of paradigm classes bearing either metonymic or metaphorical relationship to aspects of the complex concept . . . metonymic relationships underlie the indexical properties of the sign (the signifier is part of the signified, in the sense of contiguity in space and/or time and/or causality), whereas metaphorical relationships underlie iconic properties (the signifier is in some way homologous to the signified). Eisenstein's model of inner speech comprises the three principal sign-types of Peirce's typology: symbol (conventional sign . . .), icon, and index. (Eagle in Bailey et al., 1980, pp. 174–175)

In traditional art theory *material* and *form* were supposed to complement each other in harmony, with Vygotsky taking another stance:

> . . . in the course of centuries aestheticians claim the harmony of the form and the content, and that the form illustrates, complements, accompanies the content; and suddenly we discover that this is the greatest misunderstanding. Instead, the form is at war with the content, fights with it, *overcomes it*, that is this *dialectical contradiction* between the content and the form the real psychological sense of our aesthetic reactions is hidden. (Vygotsky quoted in van der Veer & Valsiner, 1991, p. 31)

---

[108]Kharitonov (1991, p. 14).

In *Psychology of Art*, Vygotsky analyzed a fable, a short story, and a tragedy. Then

> Vygotsky concluded in each case there is an affective contradiction in the psycholog-
> ical structure of a work of art. Each work causes in the individual conflicting affects
> and leads to the short-circuiting and destruction of these affects . . . Vygotsky defines
> this process as catharsis, saying that the transformation of two counterdirected affects
> constitutes the basic aesthetic response and underlies the true effect of a work of art.
> (Sobkin & Leontiev, 1992, p. 189)

The main purpose of Vygotsky's analysis of art was reflected in his belief that art is indeed the organization of future human behavior, and although the goal may never be reached it pushes us toward that which lies beyond:

> Thus the tentative schema of esthetic experience is the following: the unconscious
> impulses of the author are encoded in social, semiotic forms that appear in the text as
> its material and its formal devices. The reader experiencing this double structure of
> the text develops conflicting affective tendencies, one . . . associated with material, the
> other with the formal side. The original source . . . may also be the unconscious. The
> tension mounts and at a certain moment the reader achieves a catharsis . . . The dis-
> charge of the affect takes place in the form of intensive fantasy that restructures the
> reader's entire inner experience. (Kozulin, 1990, p. 45)

Within Vygotsky's understanding of aesthetics the principle of the dialectic is ever present, ultimately resulting in a transformation as a result of the principle of *catharsis*. The important aspect at this juncture is that many Marxist Vygotskian theoreticians remain at a lower level of dialectics, with dyads ultimately standing in opposition to each other until change is affected. The following statement is offered in the form of a hypothesis: *a higher level of dialectics is triadic (as opposed to dyadic), such as the example of Potebnya's semiotics including external sign, internal sign, signification itself (e.g., image), and the example of Peirece's semiotics divided into symbol, icon, and index. It is suggested that Vygotsky's dialectical understanding fused the following three concepts together in one aesthetic process: thesis, antithesis, and catharsis = synthesis.* This construct raises Vygotskian dialectics to a level much higher and more practical level than traditional dyadic Marxist and Hegelian philosophy. In the psychological context, Vygotsky also attempted to replace the dyadic approach with a triadic one. V. Umrikhin (1997) stated it precisely: "Hence, Vygotsky was actually proposing replacing the duality of consciousness-behavior that absorbed the attention of the other psychologists with the triad of consciousness-culture-behavior (Yaroshevsky, 1993)" (p. 26).

In analyzing the short story *Gentle Breath* or *Easy Breathing* by Ivan Bunin,[109] Vygotsky employed the oppositional forces of *thesis, antithesis, cathar-*

---

[109]Van der Veer & Valsiner (1991, p. 27). A description of the translation of the title *Gentle Breath* or *Easy Breathing* is offered. The Russian title is: *legkoe dykhanie*.

sis, and synthesis. The story builds up to the point of maximal tension reaching the breaking point, which is then transformed via catharsis. Vygotsky referred to this process as the *affective contradiction.* Ivan Bunin (1870–1954) was one of Vygotsky's favorite authors when he was a child, and *Easy Breathing* is not only an excellent point of departure for his literary analysis, but it captures Vygotsky's entire stance as it related to his scientific experiments within psychology at a later date. Blonsky (widely read by Vygotsky) was of the opinion that a text was emotionally received on the basis of the breathing rhythm of the reception of the work being read.[110] Indeed, after his university studies in Moscow in 1918, Vygotsky returned to his hometown of Gomel where he started to teach literature at a secondary school. While there he actually began psychological experiments with his students, measuring the breathing rhythms while they read Bunin's story. Another reason why *Easy Breathing* or *Gentle Breath* is an interesting choice of stories regards the fact that traditionally the study of the beginning of life is connected with breath. Sokolov (1972), for example, stated that

> ... using as a point of departure notions about a relationship between thought and words and between words and breathing, ancient thinkers used to infer that thoughts and words originated in the lungs. Thus, in the *Iliad* restless thoughts are depicted as quick moving creatures within the chest. In Plato's *Phaedrus*, Socrates says that his chest is full of thoughts. "Even for Aristotle, the substrate of thinking was the blood, as well as the Pneuma (air) and inborn heat, which imparted to the blood its higher function." ... (p. 14)

The following is the storyline of Bunin's *Gentle Breath*, following the description of Alex Kozulin (1990, p. 40). Olya Mesherskaya, a high school girl, lives a life that is no different from that of any other average, pretty, and well-to-do-girl from a provincial Russian town. Then something happens. She has a love affair with Malyutin, a landowner and friend of her father's who is much older than herself. Later she has a liaison with a Cossack officer whom she attracted and promised to wed. All this leads her astray. As a result the Cossack officer, betrayed yet still in love with Olya, shoots her in a crowded railway station. Olya's schoolmistress chooses the deceased as the subject of her passionate worship and frequently visits her grave.

Before analyzing this story and demonstrating how Vygotsky's strategy of *componential desequencing* and subsequent bricolage is relevant for the classroom, an outline is presented and divided into *disposition scheme* and *composition scheme.* "It is useful to distinguish (as many authors do) the static scheme of the construction of a narrative, which we may call its anatomy, from the dynamic scheme, which we may all its physiology" (Vygotsky, 1971, p. 149). In

---

[110]Van der Veer & Valsiner (1991, p. 30).

the case of Bunin's *Gentle Breath* the scheme appears in a parallel setting with the chronological events of the story in real time, and a listing of the events as they are unveiled in the story:

Disposition Scheme (chronological)		*Composition Scheme* (story line)	
I.	*Olia Mescherskaia*	N.	the grave
A.	childhood	A.	childhood
B.	adolescence	B.	adolescence
C.	episode with Shenshin	C.	episode with Shenshin
D.	conversation about breath	H.	last of the winter
E.	arrival of Maliutin	J.	conversation with principal
F.	liaison with Maliutin	K.	murder
G.	writing in diary	I.	episode with officer
H.	last of winter	M.	subsequent investigation
		G.	writing in diary
II.	*School Teacher*		
A.	school teaching		
B.	daydreams about brother		
C.	daydreams about great works		
D.	conversation about "gentle breath"		
E.	daydreams about Olia		
F.	walks to the cemetery		
G.	at the grave		(cf. Vygotsky, 1971, p. 151)

This particular story is rather boring from the plot line and in many respects it doesn't make much sense, never rising above any level that extends beyond daily existence, except for the tragic events. Nevertheless,

> ... the general feeling evoked in the reader of this novella is quite the *opposite* of that conveyed by the material. This resultant feeling is one of liberation. It is this light, gentle breath of the title that is the real theme of the novella, rather than the muddled life of a flirtatious schoolgirl. The main trait of the novella as a whole is "that feeling of lightness, transparency and other-worldliness which in no way can be derived from the life events of which [the story] is based". (Kozulin, 1990, pp. 41–42)

The separate episodes do not appear in the order as they would in real life. The key aspect of the murder is known from the beginning of the story, with Vygotsky discussing the fact that the word "shot" (i.e., shoot) is embedded in a long sentence, which metaphorically *muffles* the terrible act. The hidden key to the plot lies in the title *The Gentle Breath*.

> It appears at the very end, the schoolteacher's reminiscence of a conversation she once overheard, between Olia Meshcherskaia and her girl friend. . . . The "funny antique book" places the greatest emphasis on *gentle breath*. "A gentle breath! I have it, don't I? Listen, how I sigh. It's there, isn't it?" It is as if we heard the sigh ... And in this trivial description, we suddenly discover its other significance, as we

read the concluding words of the author: "And now this gentle breath is again dissi-
pated in the world, in this cloud covered sky, in this cold spring wind . . ." (Vygotsky,
1971, p. 157)

This particular example is a description of Vygotsky's understanding of
catharsis, all of which include subjective components such as emotions, the
unconscious, and the like. In fact Vygotsky felt that the story line of *Gentle Breath*
itself held an emotional background of *easy breathing* for the reader, which he
subsequently used when experimenting with his students. Vygotsky's hypothesis
was that the reader, if involved in the work, would release energy with the help
of fantasy, instead of "releasing energy in a form of action or physiological abre-
action" (Kozulin, 1990, p. 45). The concept of *fantasy* was important for Vygotsky regarding creativity, just as play is important for the same purpose in
children.[111] In *Psychology of Art*, Vygotsky also analyzed fables and *Hamlet* as
an example of a drama. Many of his ideas on semiotics were actually carried over
from this period into his writings on psychology.

By including a short summary of Vygotsky's thoughts on aesthetics it
should be remembered that this was his first love and that there is a good chance
that his works on psychology, written at a later date, were completely influenced
by aesthetics, a point often forgotten when reading Vygotsky.

CRITICISMS OF VYGOTSKY AND RESPONSES

In viewing the works of Vygotsky written mostly in the 1920s and early
1930s, it is clear that many points should be modified from a contemporary perspective. At the same time there is an attempt by some theorists to criticize
elements of the core of Vygotsky's thinking.[112] Some of these arguments are contested with the belief that Vygotsky was convinced of his position (and would
remain so today); for that reason it is felt that the core of his thoughts should
remain in tact. It is clear that since Vygotsky truly attempted to bring together an
understanding of the broadest spectrum possible in psychology–philosophy,
beginning with *consciousness*, it follows that his results would not fit into
a clearly defined understanding of traditional psychology. Before beginning
such a review of some of the basic criticisms of Vygotsky's core psychology–
philosophy, it should be understood that the most well-known Vygotskian scholars (i.e., Kozulin, van der Veer, Wertsch, Valsiner, Bakhurst, Cole, etc.) also interpret Vygotsky from their own backgrounds and perspectives; for example:

> Wertsch's text [*Vygotsky and the Social Formation of Mind (1985)*] is the finest book-
> length treatment of its subject, Western or Soviet. One of the reasons for its excellence

---

[111]For a discussion of imagination and creativity, see L. S. Vygotsky (1990). Imagination and creativity in childhood. *Soviet Psychology*. Vol. 28/1, pp. 84–96.
[112]For a good review of further criticisms of Vygotsky, see Bakhurst (1986, p. 124).

is its author's ability to speak with the authority of a participant in the debate; Wertsch absorbed himself in the Soviet tradition and arrived at his interpretation through discussions with many of Vygotsky's former collaborators (Wertsch, 1985, xiii). A consequence of this, however, is that Wertsch's presentation reproduces the Kharkovites' critique. (Bakhurst, 1996, p. 208)

Some of the major criticisms regarding tenets of Vygotsky's theories have been outlined by Wertsch and Tulviste, with the first one representing *Eurocentrism*. They feel that Vygotsky used the developmental hierarchy too broadly,[113] which appeared to afford cultural tools more importance in Europe than in other less developed countries. And although Vygotsky felt that people were biologically the same, various cultures, however, could be rated qualitatively. It should be remembered that there was a tremendous interest on the part of many researchers during the 1920s to establish a new society; and with over 120 languages in Russia, there was an effort to standardize the Russian language and allow for literacy of that language. Therefore, "one of the major challenges of a Vygotskian approach, then, is how to capture such facts about developmental progression without falling prey to ungrounded assumptions about the general superiority or inferiority of individuals of groups" (Wertsch & Tulviste, 1992, p. 554). The second major issue regards ontological development, and although Vygotsky stated that the natural and cultural lines of development merge in the child it is not exactly understood what the natural line of development meant. "This could refer to everything from the emergence of sensory abilities to motor skills to neurological development" (Wertsch & Tulviste, 1992, p. 554). The third problem area revolves around the separation of the natural and development lines of growth in the beginning stages. It appears that the natural line consists of raw materials to be transformed by the cultural line. Yet, young children are influenced by verbal social interaction from the beginning" (cf. Wertsch & Tulviste, 1992, p. 554).

Vygotsky spoke within an understanding and inclusion of aesthetics, often using metaphors to describe areas that simply could not be analyzed, then dissected and rebuilt via the scientific method. Indeed, his use of metaphoric speech is a part of the reason for the attraction Vygotsky radiates to so many readers worldwide. Within this realm, the speed he maintained in writing approximately 180 works is often forgotten, having as many as three major posts at one time, traveling across the country, often from Moscow to Petersburg to Kharkov, later to Siberia, and so on. He taught regularly, did experimental work almost constantly, had Ph.D. students, was a member of various discussion circles, lived in an apartment with many family members, had a wife and two daughters, was sick off and on from the mid 1920s, and died at the age of 37.

[113]Here is an example of one criticism of Vygotsky: "Vygotsky appeared to have a restricted view of development, essentially cognitive and a practice which appears to privilege the acquisition of the 'tool' rather than the social context of acquisition" (Daniels, 1993, p. xvii).

VYGOTSKY'S CONTRIBUTIONS

In order to give a short overview of Vygotsky's youth as a background to his contributions, Dobkin in Levitin offered a personal glimpse into Vygotsky's world:

The Vygodsky family [114] was among the most cultured in the city . . . Vygotsky was the second child in a family of eight children. He had an elder sister, four younger sisters, and two younger brothers . . . So Lev did not have a room for himself . . . Esperanto and stamp-collecting extended our horizons and brought distant countries closer. Vygotsky chose a youth in Iceland as his first penpal. We also shared a passion for chess. Vygotsky was a good player . . . What he really loved from his youth and until his last days was theatre and poetry. As long as I can remember, he was forever citing favourite verses . . . The dining-room was also a place for communication as there was invariably lively and interesting conversation during the obligatory evening tea at a large table . . . He did not enter the gymnasium (secondary school) at once . . . Vygotsky had a remarkable teacher, Solomon Ashpiz . . . Vygotsky spent two years (the seventh and eighth forms) studying at Ratner's school. It was a great change for him to emerge from a family atmosphere where he was surrounded almost exclusively by women into the company of schoolchildren . . . In the summer of 1913 our families rented dachas in Belitsa, then a suburb of Gomel. Lev was finishing the gymnasium and was already taking the so-called "deputy's exams" . . . In tsarist Russia there was a quota for the admission of Jews to institutions of higher education. This quota was three per cent at Moscow and Petersburg universities . . . He did not make a single mistake on his final exams and received a gold medal . . . Upon graduating from the University, Vygotsky returned to Gomel, and in late 1918, he and his cousin David began teaching literature at school . . . In 1924, he married Roza Smekhova, a vivacious, intelligent, pretty girl. She had a gift for staying cheerful throughout the many difficult situations in which they found themselves . . . In 1924, Vygotsky delivered a brilliant report at the Psychoneurological Congress in Petrograd which earned him an immediate invitation to come to work in Moscow . . . Vygotsky was fond of poetry as ever . . . I remember visiting Vygotsky, who was quite ill, in the last years of his life . . . Vygotsky's health grew worse. He died at the Serebryany Bor Sanatorium. (Dobkin, 1982, pp. 23–38)

Lev Semonovich and Rosa had two daughters, Gita L'vovna the oldest who is living in Moscow, and Asya, who died in 1985.[115] Some of the students of Vygotsky reported on the difficult situation in Russia in general, where there was often little to eat and much of the time it was cold inside buildings. While

[114]Vygotsky replaced the "d" in his name for "t" in the early 1920s because he believed that his name was derived from the name of the Village of Vygotovo where the family had its roots. See Dobkin (1982, p. 24).

[115]Gita L'vovna Vygodskaya reported that Asya tripped over her dog in the apartment she was living in, and that the ambulance was very late in coming to take her to the hospital which probably contributed to Asya's death in her early 50s. Interview with Dr. Vygodskaya in May 1999.

lecturing to students, he was known for pacing back and forth with his hands behind his back, often allowing his thoughts to take form in speech. It has been stated that he often had a coat on, as did the students, because of the cold.[116] Although Vygotsky only lived to be 37 it should be understood that he not only suffered physically, but he also suffered regarding the direction he saw Marxism moving toward. In particular this related to the utopian hope of a new society. Newman & Holzman (1993) recount the life of Lev Semonovich during his youth, by stating that

> first there was the extreme hardship of the post-revolutionary period—famine, the lack of other essentials . . . and of course, invasions by foreign armies and the Civil War. Vygotsky's family . . . suffered the effects. In 1918 his brother contracted tuberculosis, and in 1920, when he was 24, Vygotsky himself had the first of several serious attacks of the disease, which periodically confined him to a hospital for up to a year at a time and ultimately killed him. In addition to this kind of hardship, the calcification and distortion of Marxian practice and the abandonment of real . . . socialism . . . was another hardship . . . (p. 158)

Within the social conditions to which Vygotsky was exposed, the fact that he was Jewish perhaps played a role in his acceptance of Marxism. Within the philosophical understanding of Marxism (and perhaps Marx' own Jewish background) there was hope for a more tolerant Russia, regarding the Jewish faith under Marxism. Vygotsky's family lived in the pale (i.e., an area designated for Jews) in Gomel and it was understood that Jews could only practice certain professions. That is one reason why Vygotsky took his father's advice and started studying medicine, although his heart was not in it. He later switched to law, which was another profession that Jews were allowed to practice. In fact, simply entering the university was a stroke of luck for Lev Semonovich, although he managed to pass his examinations with a gold medal (i.e., which meant a perfect score). A tsarist law had just been passed that even Jewish gold medalists must place their names for lots to be drawn for positions at university. While studying law, Vygotsky learned the practicality of using his concept of dialectics by taking different sides in debates. These two aspects were continually used in his future works and brought him much respect with his attempt to always outline the theories and ideas of others, trying to present the position being discussed from the point of view of the opponent before giving his own solution.

Understanding the circumstances under which Vygotsky lived make his accomplishments all the more remarkable. Van der Veer & Valsiner (1991, pp. 398–399) have listed Vygotsky's major contributions to psychology as being (1) the process of dialectical synthesis, (2) a consistent developmental perspective,

---

[116]Reports from speeches given by various people whose parents or relatives studied with Vygotsky. Reports given at the Vygotsky Centennial Conference held during October 1996 at the Humanitarian University in Moscow.

(3) the method of double stimulation, and (4) an anti-reductionistic stance. As a result of the vastness of Vygotsky's works and influence, every reader would perhaps select a different point to highlight as the most meaningful aspect of his works. Worldwide interest in Vygotsky goes beyond his psychology–philosophy, including his personal ethics and life, which were a testimony to the fact that he tried to live what he wrote about.

4

Chomskyan Linguistics and Vygotskian Semiotics

American Linguistic Theory and Second Language Acquisition (SLA)

One of the paradoxes of postmodernity is the fact that in North America, with a plethora of pluralism, there has only been one dominant linguistic paradigm in place for almost 50 years, ultimately based on structuralism. Certainly there have been various European structuralist–linguistic models that could have had a lasting influence on mainstream American linguistics. For example, members of the Prague Linguistic Circle viewed functionalism from a structuralist perspective, and Helmjslev took a structuralist stance within glossematics. Why didn't these and other predominant areas of inquiry have more influence on mainstream American linguistics? It is somewhat ironic that Russian semiotics of the 1920s has caught the imagination of many scholars in various fields, while at the same time it is perceived by some Chomskyan linguists as being a threat to the *scientific method*. It is interesting to note that in returning to the origins of Saussure there was a vision of language placed within a hierarchical system, with semiotics positioned at the top of the hierarchy. The problem then revolves around an understanding of what semiotics means to linguists. In the case of de Saussure, he did not go on to investigate this field of study within the understanding of historical change. In other words, his model is static in the sense that there are no mechanisms in place to decipher the role of the individual regarding societal change. Various Russian theorists then rejected the Saussurian interpretation of linguistics during the 1920s, such as Bakhtin and Vološinov. For example,

81

> The static nature of Saussure's synchronic model and its artificial separation from the ceaselessly changing continuum of the creative flow of language was interpreted by Vološinov as the revival of the Cartesian spirit in the area of linguistic investigation ... In Russia ... Humboldtian linguistics was commonly viewed as an opposition to ... Cartesian linguistics. Thus the Humboldtian emphasis on the creative aspect of human language was identified as a typical expression of romanticism in direct opposition to modern linguistics. For Vološinov ... von Humboldt was an antithesis to Descartes and ... the most prominent antipode of abstract objectivism in European philosophy of language. (Matejka in Vološinov, 1986, pp. 167–168)

Russian linguists during the 1920s were not interested in discussions of linguistics *only* but were also vitally interested in poetry, the theater, film, semiotics, and so on. In general, one of the basic differences between contemporary American linguistics and the renaissance thinking in Russia during the 1920s is based on different philosophical positions: for example, in America, Chomskyan linguistics maintains a Cartesian understanding at the core of its philosophy, whereas in Russia most linguistic thinking during the 1920s and 1930s (the period of the writings of Vygotsky) was connected with the German philosopher and educator Wilhelm von Humboldt. At the same time it is interesting to note a similarity with Weinreich making the observation long ago that Russian linguistics has never been preoccupied with semantics;[117] however, the exception was Vygotsky who was vitally interested in semantics, writing on the development of word meaning and the semiotics of inner speech. For the most part, in Russia there has never been a feeling that semantics would solve many of the linguistic problems it faced. Another case in point regards the history of de Saussure's linguistics, which has been carried over in various forms, such as the performance/competence model. Many Russian linguists were most impressed with the work of de Saussure when Sergei Karcevskij (1884–1955) returned to Moscow in 1918 to share the linguistic understanding he had learned while studying with de Saussure in Switzerland. However, Karcevskij and many Russian linguists were quick to point out the static, linear, symmetrical relationship of Saussure's model.

In returning to the problems of the *scientific* method, there is no coincidence that in various fields (e.g., physics, philosophy, SLA, etc.) *Chaos or Complexity Theory* is slowly becoming a popular theory of explanation. This presents a challenge for the traditional understanding of the scientific method. Within the framework of *Complexity Theory* the underlying level is not chaos, but

---

[117]"It is instructive to consider some of the reasons for this discrepancy between the scope of Soviet and American linguistics. The most obvious explanation is that Soviet linguistics was never infected with the paralysis of semantic interest that caused most scholars during the Bloomfieldian period of linguistics in the United States to abdicate all semantic investigation to other (ineffectual) sciences. ... Soviet linguists as a group do not seem ever to have fallen prey to the hope that psychology (or neurology, or sociology ...) would resolve for them the difficult theoretical and methodological problems of semantic analysis" (Weinreich, 1968, pp. 60–61).

systematicity. What is truly different about this new approach is indeed the relinquishing of control, with the overall focus on the interpretation of processes (as opposed to a focus on products). The Western understanding of the Cartesian *scientific method* has been traditionally codified in the replication of various tests under different conditions with the goal of reaching the same verifiable results each time. Put simply, this approach, when implemented alone, has resulted in static output resulting in the need for *control* and to some degree *power.* The results of experiments within the Cartesian *scientific method* have usually been offered within a statistical framework lending a sense of absolutism or finality, when in reality the results can change over time. Within a contextualized approach to linguistics, some of the most interesting variables needed for explanation have been automatically eliminated, such as volition, emotion, motivation, image, and so on. Without including nonverifiable aspects of human behavior into the Cartesian *scientific method* it is somewhat paradoxical that the conclusions drawn will ultimately be *relative* and not *absolute.* H. G. Widdowson (1990), for example, stated that

> we should recognize that the validity of research findings is always *relative*, and relative in two quite different ways. First it is relative to the conditions which are imposed on a particular empirical inquiry. It does not follow that if subjects are induced to behave in a certain way within the idealized limits of experimental control, they will behave in the same way when these limits are relaxed. In a sense, experimental subjects are only partially real people. (p. 25)

In general, the problem of the Cartesian scientific method results in a somewhat inflexible approach to Chomskyan linguistics. Certainly one of the basic functions of linguistics should be to serve as a theoretical conduit for understanding language acquisition and language learning. However, Chomskyan linguistics is not contributing to this area as has been anticipated. Larsen-Freeman listed some of the reasons why the influence of American linguistics has declined within SLA in the past few years.[118] One of the main problems revolves around the claim by some linguists to a Cartesian *scientific method*, while defending the Chomskyan linguistic paradigm with quasi-religious fervency. Another problem of American linguistic theory has often resulted in a unidirectional approach to language, with the innatist tendency ironically implying a determinist positioning, whether willingly or not.

---

[118]"Let me now attempt to answer the question why the influence of linguistics has declined. . . . First, linguistic theories have become increasingly abstract over the years. . . . Second, much of mainstream linguistics deals with the formal properties of language abstracted from context, not the meaningful use of language . . . The third reason has to do with the perceived character of linguistic knowledge as contrasted with the nature of language teaching. . . . Fourth, where the notion of language undergoes periodic redefinition by linguists, teachers need to entertain competing views of language simultaneously. . . . They [teachers] cannot afford to subscribe to one theory of language" (Larsen-Freeman, 1995, pp. 720–721).

Within postmodernity it is difficult to believe that there is one theory of linguistics, one competency, one proficiency, one grammar, one path to follow. Singular and detached domains, which exist independently of each other, no longer fit within a worldview of separate-but-connected. Multiple, connected models are now emerging (such as Chaos–Complexity Theory) that interface, lending a sense of dynamism and three dimensionality to existing one-dimensional positions. In understanding the salience of Vygotskian thought a caveat needs to be discussed. As a Spinozian universalist, Vygotsky viewed holism as a convergence of lines of development, all of which have different origins, different directions, and so forth. In other words, Vygotskian holism does not refer to the isomorphic unification of dialectical opposites. Within the Vygotskain understanding emphasis is placed on the developmental emergence of *engagements* and *separations* joining within different levels of consciousness. There is a view of dialectical understanding and development, infused with external, societal meaning, and there exist separate systems functioning on different levels. However, there is also the monistic understanding of connectedness at a deeper (or higher) plane, with varying levels of consciousness functioning together. In other words, spaces are opening up for multilevel explanations of linguistic systems and language acquisition, instead of singular and independent responses. Evelyn Hatch et al. (1990) called for the need of an integrated theory by stating that

> as we think about our experiences as teachers and researchers and examine our beliefs about the learning process, it becomes clear that we have no all-encompassing theory of language acquisition that matches what we have learned from experience. Rather, we find a great deal of research on small parts of the total picture without an integrated theory to guide our work. (p. 697)

What is paradoxical is that the Chomskyan model is ultimately based on intuition and is situated within highly abstract mathematical parameters. The question arises as to whether Chomskyan linguistics can actually operate within the traditional mode of inductive (bottom-up) research, when its overall tenets remain at the deductive level (top down).

At this point a caveat should be given: there is absolutely no call to simply replace *one theory with another theory*, or to replace Chomskyan linguistics with Vygotskian semiotics. Chomskyan linguistics does not deal with real time, and according to Chomsky, his theories have little applicability to the classroom pedagogy of language learning/acquisition. On the other hand, Vygotsky's theories were written with a view to restructuring the educational experience. There is, however, a call to go beyond "agreeing to disagree," meaning that all linguists should be familiar with linguistic systems different from the Chomskyan model. For example, Halliday presents his understanding of grammar within a socialized context, whereas Chomsky presents his theories within an idealized framework; Krashen represents an innatist linguistic understanding of L2 acquisition, whereas

Bialystock speaks within a cognitive understanding;[119] Eckman offers a linguistic interpretation of markedness, whereas Kellerman writes on markedness from a psycholinguistic point of view, and so on. The purpose of this section is to offer thoughts on language from a Vygotskian semiotic perspective, directly compared with the Chomskyan philosophical underpinnings. This comparison should be viewed from a metaphorical, as well as a metatheoretical perspective. A direct comparison cannot be made because one theory deals with "real" time and the other theory deals with the "idealized" situation.

Within Chomskyan theory the focus of research was initially located within the model of the English (or better, American) language. Since many researchers and teachers in Second Language Acquisition often teach and research in languages other than English, especially within the applied linguistic sociocultural tradition, this fact precludes the need of going beyond the acceptance of an English-based linguistic theory.

The Chomskyan model, which represents a *nonconstrained rationality*, tends to establish territorial hegemony with a fierce battle in maintaining perceived hierarchies. This section offers a summary of selected aspects of Chomskyan linguistics from a philosophical perspective, connecting it with Vygotskian semiotic theories, which will lead into the "Fodor Paradox." The discussion turns towards "Fodor–Whorf–Vygotsky" for a better understanding of the range of opinions represented, from innatism to relativism to universalism. The next section views three areas from a Chomskyan perspective with the three topics being reviewed again in the same order from a Vygotskian perspective. These areas are *rationalism, innatism, and competence*. It is hypothesized that a basic understanding of Chomskyan linguistics represents a mathematical exercise in attempting to formulate language within algorithmic structures, although it is commonly held that the approach is heuristic. With that in mind, the Vygotskian framework does not offer a theory of language *per se*, but is semiotic in nature by placing sign systems, *word meaning as a unit of analysis*, concept formation, and the like within *a genetic (here: starting point)–developmental asymmetrical continuum*.[120] It also focuses on the internal processes of individual learning related to the overall societal framework. The Vygotskian understanding of *consciousness–psychology–philosophy–semiotics* is in a position of offering direct, heuristic applications to both linguistic theory and to the L2 classroom pedagogy. A Vygotskian approach focuses on the potential development of the learner within

---

[119]See Ellis (1994, p. 355).

[120]"Calling his psychology 'developmental' (geneticheskii—from genesis), Vygotsky meant much more than a mere analysis of the unfolding of behavior in ontogenesis. As a matter of fact, the very idea of development as unfolding and as maturation was alien to him. Vygotsky perceived psychological development as a dynamic process full of upheavals, sudden changes, and reversals. This process, however, ultimately leads to the formation of the cultural, higher mental functions" (Kozulin, 1986, p. 266).

the *Zone of Proximal Development*. As well it focuses on the *general genetic law of development*, that is, "any function in the child's cultural development appears twice or on two planes . . . It appears first between people as an intermental category, and then within the child as an intramental category" (Vygotsky, 1987, p. 21), which includes aspects such as *cultural mediation, personal appropriation or internalization*, and above all *concept development*. Within the Vygotskian stance it is understood that the traditional view of the *mind* is mostly a social rather than an individual construct and that learning is placed within the constraints of both the *lower mental processes* (i.e., natural conditioned reflexes, such as perception and involuntary attention) and *higher mental processes* (i.e., culturally nonconditioned responses, such as voluntary memory). A basic tenet of Vygotskian psychology–philosophy is that background knowledge and overall development must be in place for new concepts to be internalized via semiotic mediation, and that the normal procedure of *associative learning will never lead to genuine concept formation within the higher mental processes*. Certainly associative learning represents an integral part of the lower levels of mental processing, and this aspect can be found in much SLA research, such as vocabulary learning, to use one example.[121] Much (not all) research on vocabulary learning represents an example of the atomistic approach taken in SLA research, where words and word acquisition are often studied without regard to context or to linguistic development. This analogy can apply to other areas and can even serve as a metaphor regarding the approach often taken regarding human cognition within language production. In other words, much of Chomskyan SLA has dealt with lower levels of mental functions in designing a theory of language, via innatism; within that model there has been a lack of inclusion of the dialectic, or asymmetry, or simple weighting between valences, which are ultimately necessary for change and development. To put it succinctly, much of the Chomskyan model is static. The following points represent just a couple of the problems within the Chomskyan understanding: language is equated with sentences that are then discussed one at a time; before the Minimalist approach adjectives were treated as cases of ellipsis; there is confinement of meaning to the lexicon; no aspect of metaphor is accounted for; and many of the irregularities which remained problems within the 1980s Government Binding period have simply been labeled "marked."[122]

Therefore, it is claimed that an eclectic approach used to place Chomsky and Vygotsky together would be wrongheaded. However, there is a place on the same continuum[123] of human languages for both theories, and indeed, there could

---

[121]For a discussion of associationism and behaviorism, see Talyzina (1961, pp. 226–318).

[122]Some of the points listed were adapted from Robinson (1975, pp. 36–51). Also refer to Botha (1989, pp. 86–87).

[123]In speaking about the crisis in Psychology in the 1920s, Vygotsky argued that there was ultimately one continuum for psychology, where all of the theories of psychology would fit. This was not a

be more collaboration in order to better understand the positioning of both sides. As A. A. Leontiev (in Wertsch, 1978) stated: ". . . neither a one-sided semiotic nor a one-sided linguistic approach to language can reveal its essential nature, no matter how precise the analysis" (p. 24). Within the following discussion on *rationalism, innatism,* and competence, the reader should understand that earlier Chomskyan theories are discussed, many of which were discarded not to be replaced, such as deep structure and competence. Although many of the earlier Chomskyan theories are no longer cited within current Chomskyan research, the reason for dismissing them from Government Binding, the Minimalist Program, *inter alia,* does not explain what has replaced them. Were these theories not correct? Is there no deep structure? No competence? No D- or S-structure? No government, which is referred to as an "arbitrary syntactic relation"? Are the A- from A-bar positions no longer basic? No creativity? Were earlier theories too difficult to explain? Are they no longer worthy of discussion?[124] And within the Minimalist Program we now have a new list of terminology, such as *relativized minimality, procrastinate, computational system, spell-out, converge, crash, checking, merge, minimal link condition, greed,* and so on. Also within the Minimalist Program the necessary components are LF (semantic component) and PF (phonetic component), with the needed aspects of *lexicon* and *computational system.* The entire outlay of the system resembles the analogy of placing human language within a computer model of understanding, including *interface conditions.* Here is an example of the new language from V. Cook and M. Newson (1996): "Specifically, semantic information is not allowed to appear at PF and phonetic information is not allowed to appear at LF. A derivation **converges** at each of the interface levels if such conditions are met, otherwise it **crashes**" (p. 321).

The approach taken here is philosophical and uses Chomskyan terms from different periods of his works, sometimes indiscriminately. A generalized framework would take 1957 as the beginning of Generative Grammar, into the Standard Theory of the 1960s, and into the Extended Standard Theory up through the 1970s. The 1980s were strongly connected with the period of Government Binding, and the 1990s with the Minimalist Program. Most of these periods simply delete previous problems, often excluding them, to add on new areas of focus. Vygotsky, on the other hand, is noted for the continuity of his theories from the very beginning to the end (certainly with exceptions as well), spanning multiple interdisciplinary fields. Chomsky's approach can be viewed in the following way: "A more productive approach might be to treat him [Chomsky] like a great and restless artist—like Picasso, with his postimpressionist period, his blue

---

theory of modularity, but a developmental design from the lower to the higher aspects, with both poles of the continuum being necessary for the whole, and with the higher aspects serving the function of a measuring stick for the lower areas.

[124]Refer to V. Cook et al. (Eds.) (1996, pp. 314–316).

period, his rose period, his cubist period . . ." (Harris, 1993, p. 233). Terence Moore and Christine Carling (1987, pp. 26–27) have given another example when using Isaiah Berlin's discussion of *The Hedgehog and the Fox*, which was taken from a story by Tolstoy. The Greek poet Archilocus stated: *The fox knows many things, but the hedgehog knows one big thing.* "If we consider our own field, it seems to us that Chomsky is an innate hedgehog with a hedgehog's longings" (Moore & Carling, 1987, p. 26). With that introduction, it is time to begin the summary of rationalism, innatism, and competence from two different perspectives.

Rationalism (Chomskyan Perspective)

The starting point for this discussion is not linguistics per se, but *rationalism*, on which Chomskyan thought is based. In equating rationalism with Descartes it is worthwhile to remember that the 17th century was very different from the 20th century, as simplified as that sounds. Rationalism was a manifested belief in solving human problems with technical answers, as nature solves its own problems through consistent universal laws. When reading Descartes today, one is struck by his reference to God on so many pages and his bridge between body and mind being the soul, which he conjectured to be situated within the pineal gland. Descartes wrote:

> Let us then conceive here that the soul has its principal seat in the little gland which exists in the middle of the brain, from whence it radiates forth through all the remainder of the body by means of the animal spirits, nerves, and even the blood, which participating in the impressions of the spirits, can carry them by the arteries into all the members. (Vesey, 1964, p. 47)

The esoteric quality of language of the 17th century is now forgotten when speaking of Descartes, as is reference to the brutality of those times, such as witch hunts. The result of this thinking attributed *consciousness* and thought to the realm of the human mind, not human body, with these attributes taking on static, rather than dynamic qualities. One of the basic components of Descartes' thought was that "truth" couldn't be understood by perception, thereby generating much discussion on intuition. Two of the basic qualities attributed to Descartes' understanding of rationalism are the individual and mathematics used in problem solving. These two positions placed together have afforded a paradoxical understanding of unlimited hope in technological progress, and at the same time, they have placed the individual in a quasi-passive state of being via innateness. Descartes felt that the mind has two modes of thought: both perception and the operation of understanding are passive, according to Descartes, while volition, or will, remain active (cf. Marková & Foppa, 1990, p. 60). A misconception could arise that scholars, such as Humboldt and others, believed in a nonmathematical orientation to human ontology. Basilius (1952) confronted the issue of the followers of Humboldt long before Chomsky became popular by stating that

> the stance of the Neo-Humboldtians is both mentalistic and psychologistic but their approach and method are nonetheless empirical. They are in conscious opposition to traditional linguistics including the contemporary American variety on the grounds that it has operated in a social vacuum by continuing to restrict itself exclusively to the formalogical analysis of languages. (p. 98)

For example, Vygotsky was in essence a follower of the Humboldtian tradition and he firmly believed in objectifying internal processes as much as possible, to be analyzed within a scientific–Spinozian approach. One of the major differences between followers of the tradition established by Descartes and of that established later by Humboldt was the difference in understanding mathematics and rationalism. Vološinov gave a cogent statement on the position of enlightenment–rationalism from a linguistic and a Russian perspective:

> The idea of the *conventionality, the arbitrariness of language*, is a typical one for rationalism as a whole, and no less typical is the *comparison of language to the system of mathematical signs*. What interests the mathematically minded rationalists is not the relationship of the sign to the actual reality it reflects nor to the individual who is its originator, but the *relationship within a closed system* already accepted and authorized. (Vološinov, 1986, pp. 57–58)[125]

[125]In solving the long-standing problem of whether Bakhtin or Vološinov wrote *Marxism and the Philosophy of Language* it has been stated: "Why did he [Bakhtin] refuse to acknowledge these books as his own? First of all, because there was much in them to which he would not have signed his name. . . . Why did he renounce it? First of all because it did not satisfy him. Moreover, after he had already acknowledged his authorship, he told me that Medvedev   introduced certain additions, and 'they were very unsuccessful,' said Bakhtin. Moreover, these books were not written with the same refinement as say the book on Dostoevsky. He dictated them. And he told me straight out . . . that he wrote them simply for the money" (Rzhevsky, 1994, pp. 430–431). For more explanations see: "Vološinov, Ideology, and Language: The Birth of Marxist Sociology from the Spirit of *Lebensphilosophie*." Galin Tihanov, *The South Atlantic Quarterly* (1998, 97/3–4, pp. 599–622). Bakhtin did not establish a dialectical tension, locating the Hegelian dialectic within the realm of the abstract with statement such as: "In dialogue we take out the voices (the division of voices), we take out the intonations (personal and emotional), concepts and abstract judgments are drawn from the living words and responses, all is mixed inside a single abstract consciousness and this is how we obtain dialectics" (Ponzio, 1992, p. 395). In other words, Bakhtin's project focused on the whole and not so much on elements of the whole situated within dialectics. Bakhtin's reference to *dialogue* and *inner speech* are somewhat different from Vygotsky's, but the inclusion of such terms shows the *discourse worlds* of intellectual circles in Russia in the 1920s. It should be remembered that Vygotsky's ultimate interest was in aesthetics and educational psychology, while Bakhtin's ultimate interest was in literature. In some respects, Bakhtin was anti-dialectic: "The dialectic development of a single spirit according to relations of thesis, antithesis and synthesis is absent, there is no tension towards a single and definitive conclusion for which all the various parts of the work must be functional. The very object of Bachtin's research makes the application of dialectics of Hegelian type inappropriate . . ." (Ponzio, 1992, p. 395).

The algorithmic tradition for Descartes was mechanistic, used in part to comprehend the laws of nature; for Vygotsky, following Humboldt, this tradition was used to better understand science beginning with the lower levels of mental functions, later incorporating the principles of heuristics within the higher levels of mental processing.

Innatism (Chomskyan Perspective)

There is often a misunderstanding of how Descartes interpreted the word *innatism*, which was understood as *a capacity of the mind, not of ideas*:

> Descartes spoke of ideas as being innate, strictly speaking it was not the ideas that were innate, but the faculty of the mind producing them. Consequently, he did not consider that innate ideas existed fully-fledged in a baby's mind. (Marková, 1982, p. 42)

Descartes did not mean to equate innatism with ideas, rather with the faculty of the mind that produces ideas. For Chomsky, it is the *modular mental structure* that is considered to be innate. Now, Chomsky also takes up the issue of a baby not having innate ideas, and with an extension of this argument it is then understood that for everyone, "innate principles of language acquisition may never be present in conscious thought" (Leiber, 1975, p. 168). The problem slowly begins to evolve with a hypothetical position that if ideas in the mind of a child are not innate from birth, then they must require experience in order to develop. For example:

> if innate ideas are latent in that they require experience to bring them out, then they are not like being endowed with legs and arms ... This raises the need to make quite clear how the claim of innate knowledge ... is distinguishable from the claim of empiricism. For if experience is stipulated as a necessary condition for exhibiting both innate knowledge and principles ... we need criteria for choosing between these two hypotheses. The rationalist will have to show that the particular experiences he believes necessary for eliciting innate knowledge cannot ... account for the knowledge he claims is innate. (Zimmerman, 1969, p. 199)

The point being made here is that Chomksyan cognitivists need to offer a more precise definition of their position on innatism to better explain their core beliefs in general. At this stage in the discussion many questions are raised, such as, What does *innate* actually mean? Is there truly an understanding that the human telos will unfold in behavior over time without an individualized social–experiential base? Is only the mind capable of innateness, or do the ideas actually contain elements of innateness? This brings up the question about the LAD that was popular years ago, namely, what is it? Without a clear, concise understanding of the Chomskyan position it must be assumed from his writings that human nature is for the most part predetermined. Now, there is no argument that part of the human makeup is innate, certainly there is agreement with Schlesinger's (in Rivers, 1983) view, which maintains that "there can be no question . . . that the organism comes to any learning task with some innate equipment; the question is only how much is innate. The soundest approach seems to make as few assumptions as possible, and to try to explain with these as much as possible" (p. 91). A problem in Chomyskan linguistics is that if one applies the concept of falsification, then aspects such as innatism cannot be disproved. Douglas Brown quotes Ambrose Bierce in using a dictionary definition of "innate": "The doctrine of innate ideas is one of the most admirable faiths. A philosophy, being itself an innate idea and therefore inaccessible to disproof . . ." (Brown, 1987, p. 9). It has been claimed that the innatism Chomsky sees in child L1 learning is somewhat derived from contextual cues, an assumption that contains the following problem:

> I suggest that the need for "innate ideas" rests on the false premise that the phonetic form of utterance is the *only* information on which the child might base generalizations. The latter premise stems from the assumption that language is self-contained. When language use is taken into account, the phonetic form of utterances is obviously not the only information available to the child. The utterances which he observes occur in contexts that are rich in situational information. Words and sentences are observed to relate to persons, events, objects, and relations in a systematic way. (Oller, 1973, p. 38)

Similar problems of innatism can be discussed in relation to the older term *competence*, which in many respects disappeared from the later writings of Chomsky, not to be replaced. This problem will never be resolved and might be identified with the position of Plato, where the abstract model of mathematics and logic was applied to the ideals of various aspects of life, while not entering the realm of the concrete.

Competence (Chomskyan Perspective)

After briefly reviewing rationalism and innateness, another area of difference in thinking is that of *competence*. Even though this term it is no longer discussed within Chomskyan linguistics it appears to be a notion worthy of debate. Competence is (or was) viewed as being *a priori*, in opposition to performance. "The basic condition for the understanding of language, he [Chomsky] maintains, is 'competence,' and only 'competence' can provide accurate linguistic 'performance'" (Luria, 1974–75, p. 380); however, "Chomsky himself recognized and stated that linguistic rules cannot define performance rules, but performance processes must include linguistic descriptions of a competence theory"

(Leuninger, 1975, p. 196). What becomes paradoxical is that *competence*, residing in the subconscious, cannot be described; however, the Cartesian search for answers certainly has led to an alogrithmic approach of knowledge which lends itself to mathematical formulations, with a "yes–no" stance. At the same time, "there is no such thing as a 'yes–no' approach in the Hegelian framework" (Marková, 1982, p. 178), a position adopted in part by Vygotsky. Now, what follows is that

> if one thus describes the object of linguistic study as the rule system that explains the implicit knowledge of the speaker–hearer, and the object of study of psycholinguistics as the analysis of rule-guided behavior that underlies communicative processes, then the question of adequate methods of description for these two different rule types arises out of this difference, for "algorithmic procedures of sentence derivation cannot function as models for language behavior, because they cannot function in real time". (Bartsch & Rennemann, 1975, p. 197)

It is at this point that a fundamental problem arises relating to the relationship of mathematics and linguistics. Slama-Cazacu (in Bain, 1983) is one voice among many who claims that "linguistics cannot be identified with mathematics. Mathematical models can ignore a psychological reality whereas linguistic models cannot" (p. 262). Chomskyan linguistics cannot be understood to be truly psychological by simply stating the connection between mathematics and linguistics without an adequate model of the concrete individual within a socialized context.

The question then arises as to a definition of competence—is it more than the sum of performances? A. R. Luria has made a similar statement to that of Courtney Cazden (1972) with the argument running as follows:

> Consequently, we must consider that linguistic "competence" which Chomsky believes is intuitive, is in actual fact the result of a long and dramatic evolution and is a problem rather than a postulate. Furthermore, we should assume that "competence" is the result of long and dramatic "performances" which were endowed with prelinguistic characteristics from the start, but which acquired their linguistic traits during the young child's early contact with the speaking environment . . . Language is thus a system of codes used to express the relations of the subject with the outside world. (Luria, 1974–1975, p. 383)

Some basic questions now arise based on the past arguments that relate to the surface and deep structure:

1. The relationship between the surface and deep structure is not always the same. Not only is there no element of real time within the deep structure, but there is also no understanding of movement, or change (i.e., dialectic, hence, no asymmetrical component). Luria gave an example where special transformations are required, with ambiguous sentences within the surface structure being the same, while the deep structure remains different:

As an example, take the two sentences examined in detail both by Chomsky and Khomskaya (1958). Khomskaya analyzed the process whereby children comprehend the
sentences "Petya predlozhil yabloko" (Peter offered an apple) and "Petya poprosil
yabloko" (Peter requested an apple). These two sentences appear to have identical
structures. However, their deep syntactic structures turn out to be quite different. In
the first sentence, the subject (Peter) is clearly an agent, and this is represented in the
surface structure in a direct way. The semantic structure of this sentence is revealed
by reading from left to right. The second sentence, however, involves another person
who is not explicitly named. It can be rephrased as "Petya poprosil, chtoby *kto-nibud'*
dal emu yabloko." (Peter requested that *someone* give him an apple). That is, it must
be comprehended from right to left (someone will give Peter an apple which he is
expecting). This clearly emerges from the deep syntactic structure of the second sentences . . . Where the surface structures of sentences are identical, the difference in
their meaning is revealed only by analyzing their deep syntactic structure. (Luria, 1981,
p. 124)

Chomsky never fully accounted for these mistakes from 1957, which
brought on two more problems: for the deep structure to remain *deep*, it had to
remain incapable of further analysis; and if it were incapable of any further analysis how would it retain the criteria of being *deep* within its own mathematically
oriented logic? As a result of the first premise everything of significance must
then be analyzable on the surface structure, which was supposed to result in the
discovery of the deep structure,[126] with the entire model becoming circular. A criticism of this strategy has been offered by John M. Ellis (1993):

But with "deep structure" . . . the reference point of *everything* now seemed to be
semantic content. "Deep structure" seemed indeed to be a factual semantic core, for it
was hard to talk of the transformations that resulted in surface structure (that is, the
actual shape of a real piece of language) without talking of the addition of meaning
elements (for example, interrogative transformations) or the alleged nonaddition of
meaning elements (as in passive transformations). Chomsky had implicitly reversed
his earlier position, but because of a determination not to concede error it was a reversal clouded in double-talk. (p. 103)

2.   The second issue arising from the debate on *competence* then revolves
around "langue" and "parole." These concepts were taken out of their intentional settings instantiated by de Saussure and were then rewritten/restructured
by Chomsky within an idealized psychological framework. It has been hypothesized that

Chomsky's attempt to rewrite this distinction [competence and performance] only confused it, and his reason for doing so was both dangerous and unnecessary: because
"performance" (i.e., actual speech) might contain errors, we need to "idealize" the data
to reach the abstraction "competence." (Ellis, 1993, p. 104)

Of course, the major betrayal for some generative linguists came in the
late 1960s with generative semantics, where attempts were made to analyze the

---

[126]cf. Ellis (1993, p. 103).

semantic core of competence. The argument reaches closure with many statements having been made along the following lines:

> He [Chomsky] also suggests that the ultimate knowledge is uniform, if not fixed, even if the original data is not. But this raises the problem of the distinction that Chomsky draws between competence and performance. Competence represents a measure of the child's ultimate knowledge of language, since Chomsky equates competence with what the speaker actually knows, whereas performance represents what the speaker reports about his knowledge (the actual use of language in concrete situations) . . . (Zimmerman, 1969, p. 205)

In general, it is agreed with Luria that assuming deep structures are innate makes a postulate out of a problem. Simply "doing away" with the competence/performance model without redefining it or replacing with another model does not mean that discussion of this problem needs to cease. The question has been posed as to whether factors shaping language are then specific to language, or whether they are general features of the learning apparatus.[127] There is no attempt to take the argument further at this point, including the implications of possible fossilized grammatical mistakes of native speakers, nor is there any attempt here to even discuss the position of the native speaker, which has traditionally represented the status quo; there is no mentioning of the problems in trying to make Chomskyan linguistics "scientific" nor of the fact that although Chomsky has had a near monolithic influence on SLA research. Chomsky himself stated that his ideas were not adequate for second language pedagogy.[128] Some of these points are discussed under the section on Universal Grammar; however, the important issue at this stage is to reach a modified closure, returning to the initial summary within a Vygotskian understanding of Chomskyan linguistics. In order to complete such an analysis the same topics of *rationalism*, *innatism*, and *competence* are viewed within a Vygotskian approach. The areas of relativity, together with representationalism and perception, are also viewed within a summary approach.

VYGOTSKIAN UNDERSTANDING OF RATIONALISM, INNATISM, COMPETENCE

Rationalism (Vygotskian Perspective)

In beginning this summary of differences between a Vygotskian and Chomskyan understanding of language the initial starting point of *rationalism* is taken

---

[127]cf. Schwartz (1969, p. 189).

[128]Chomsky stated in 1968: "my own feeling is that from our knowledge of the organization of language and of the principles that determine language structure one cannot immediately construct a

up once again. It should be remembered that Vygotsky's primary concern regarding his semiotics was the educational application of his theories. With that in mind the initial understanding of rationalism is that

> ultimately, the Vygotskian position presupposes a different conception of rationality. In this conception, rationality does not coincide with formal logic or with the adequate use of "objective," decontextualized knowledge. Rationality would have to be seen as bound to situated activity, as plural, and as political. What a pluralist theory of education needs is a theory of the historical genesis of rationality, which speaks to the relationship between the private and the public sphere, between the development of the person and that of society . . . Transmission of objectified knowledge has displaced personality formation as the aim of education. (Wardekker, 1996, pp. 2–4)

The position here does not parallel the European postmodern debate of the 1980s between Lyotard in France and Habermas in Germany, with Lyotard supporting a return to the "large narrative" (métarécits) with a longing for an older world structure and a recapturing of the "rhythm" of the universe. This stance denies the telos of rationality as containing the ultimate answers of humanity being positioned within technology. On the other side of the debate, Habermas takes the position that the project of modernity has not yet been completed and that rationality has not reached the final stages of technological development. He is of the opinion that one day people will be capable of solving many of the problems in the world, assuming that the tenets of "morality" are reinfused into the basic understanding of science and technology. In many respects, at least on a theoretical level, Vygotsky has supplied both criteria for a new rationality, one with the aesthetic feel for the rhythm of the universe, with his internal longing for higher culture through poetry, theater, and so forth; at the same time, Vygotsky firmly believed in using the Spinozian, scientific/interpretative method for the purpose of solving societal problems. This approach might sound paradoxical to many, and that is perhaps the reason why James Wertsch has labeled Vygotsky the "ambivalent enlightenment rationalist":

> There seems to be a side to him [Vygotsky] that was committed to the standard account of the Enlightenment (Toulmin, 1992) which viewed abstract rationality as superseding irrational dogmatism and other pitfalls associated with pre-Enlightenment times . . . At the same time . . . there seems to be [a] side of Vygotsky that recognized the power of human thinking and action grounded in the harmony of the imagination . . . and other phenomena that do not fit neatly into standard accounts of the Enlightenment and its descendants. . . . it is important to remember that Vygotsky did not associate these phenomena with irrationality . . . or other such labels. (Wertsch, 1995b, pp. 56–57)

teaching programme. All we can suggest is that a teaching programme be designed in such a way as to give free play those creative principles that humans bring to the process of language learning, and I presume to the learning of anything else. I think we should probably try to create a rich linguistic environment for the intuitive heuristics that the normal human automatically possesses" (Christophersen, 1973, p. 19).

Vygotsky offered solutions to the intrinsic problem of traditional rational-ism, serving as a bridge between those "for and against" the project of rational-ist–enlightenment. Van der Veer & Valsiner (1991) have taken this point and traced it back to Spinoza, stating that "thus, Spinoza combined his ideal of a ratio-nal man with a notion of intellectual tools that was not unlike Vygotsky's . . . We may conclude, then, that Vygotsky defended an image of rational man who had learned to submit his primitive drives and emotions to the control of intellect" (p. 241). In returning to Spinoza, it is appropriate to allow his words to stand as they were in 1677:

> But as men at first made use of the instruments supplied by nature to accomplish very easy pieces of workmanship . . . and then . . . wrought other things more difficult with less labour and greater perfection; and so gradually mounted from the simplest oper-ations to the making of tools . . . till they arrived at making . . . the vast number of com-plicated mechanisms which they now possess. So . . . the intellect . . . makes for itself intellectual instruments, whereby it acquires strength for performing other intellectual operations, and from these operations gets again fresh instruments . . . and thus grad-ually proceeds till it reaches the summit of wisdom. (Spinoza, 1955 [1677], p. 12)

A problem which is yet to be solved is the appropriacy of using scientific methods in analyzing internal, higher mental processes. For example, Peeter Tulviste (1991) has made a somewhat controversial statement along these lines claiming that "both the signs themselves and the way they are used have a cultural, not a natural origin, and for this reason the higher mental processes, as distinct from the lower, are subject only to cultural–historical and not natural-scientific explanation" (p. 30). This interpretation is open to tremendous contro-versy. Certainly this point of view can represent a possible Vygotskian position, minus the fact that Vygotsky viewed both the lower and higher mental functions as residing within one asymmetrical (not contiguous) continuum (understood within Spinozian monism). To be sure, even this statement alone is contested by many experts within the Vygotskian tradition. The claim here is that Vygotsky's understanding of Spinoza lends to this interpretation, but there is no attempt to prove this postulate one way or the other. Vygotsky himself would be the only person able to answer this question, and no one knows what he would think today. These statements quickly become emotionally charged, with fervent believers on each side of the debate.

One of the interesting solutions to the complexity of the rationalist–enlight-enment debate is to be found within a more eclectic approach. For example, it is intuitively known that the only answer to overwhelming societal problems is the advancement of a more "enlightened" approach to technology, using a more enhanced "eco-" framework. Lauren Resnick (in Cole, 1996) has coined a term that synthesizes the problem in general, called the *situated rationalist*.

> By situated Resnick means a loose collection of theories and perspectives that propose a contextualized and social view of the nature of thinking and learning. By rationalist

she means the theories that claim a prior biological constraints on the development of domain-specific knowledge. . . . (p. 217)

Certainly it is fair to say that Vygotsky's thoughts were so future-oriented and interdisciplinary that it is almost impossible to find a single label for him. All of the labels regarding rationalism consistently remain insufficient.

Innatism (Vygotskian Perspective)

Although Vygotsky's comprehension of "innatism" is often misunderstood and sometimes misrepresented, it is important to establish that he indeed believed that the lower mental processes were innate. Perhaps he would have revised his thoughts if he were living today. This understanding coincides with the establishment of one continuum, where the lower mental processes reside on one end of the continuum, with the higher mental functions–capacities–processes residing on the other. However, these processes do not *function* as one entity. With the hypothesis that Vygotsky would have supported a "one continuum" theory, it should be understood that the origins of various processes, such as thinking and speech, maintain different roots and directions. One *continuum* does not imply that all stages of development; all functions, and the like have the same origin or the same trajectory of growth. There is no value-laden perspective suggesting a preference for any single position (lower or higher mental processes), since both are mutually nonexclusive, each needing the other for development. This brings up the position that even innate factors can be influenced by the higher mental processes, just as monism can be influenced by the *dialectic* or as *meaning* can be influenced by *sense*. For example, in referring to the external and the semantic aspects of speech, the higher mental processes are based on the lower mental processes and the lower mental functions, according to Vygotsky, need to be organized so that they are viewed and analyzed from the higher perspective. At the same time,

> analysis shows that the lower form is the basis and content of the higher form, that the higher form appears only at a certain stage of development and in turn itself continuously passes into the lower form. However, the problem is not limited to this, since if we should want to limit ourselves exclusively to analysis or reducing the higher form to the lower, we would never be able to develop an adequate representation of all the specific features of the higher form and those patterns to which they are subordinate. (Vygotsky in Rieber, 1997, p. 81)

This was perhaps the essence of what Vygotsky meant when he stated that "the anatomy of man is the key to the anatomy of the ape" (Bakhurst, 1986, p. 107). This understanding coincides with Vygotsky's personal and professional attempt at viewing oneself and others within the highest possible explanatory principle possible. As well, this type of understanding represents an inextricable part of the human condition, meaning that "reflexes–responses" are simply a *sine qua non* of the makeup of all human activity. On the side of the lower mental functions one finds the model of "stimulus–response" or conditioned reflexes, with the unconditioned reflexes residing on the higher level of the asymmetrical, dialectical (both dyadic and triadic) continuum. These responses represent the makeup of everyday life for each human being, which are culturally mediated via semiotic signs, *inter alia*. Before moving on it is important to reiterate that the understanding of one continuum parallels the planet earth, metaphorically speaking. Although there are different nations, cultures, languages, needs, and so on, all people have the planet earth as their common denominator. This idea does not mean to imply that *continuum equals sameness*. This implies that not only the earth influences people living on it, but also the earth is influenced by the actions and intentions of its inhabitants.

Innatism and the Fodor Paradox

At this stage an introductory analysis of the extreme innatist position, the *Fodor paradox*, is given, starting from the question, *Do the higher level processes develop from lower levels or not*? Chomsky stated that "If we give up the idea that higher levels are literally constructed out of lower level elements, as I think we must, then it becomes much more natural to consider even such abstract systems of representation as transformational structure . . ." (Chomsky, 1961, p. 43). Vygotsky and Luria, in contrast, felt that

> the idea of development proves here to be the key to the comprehension of the unity of all psychological functions, and, at the same time, of the inception of higher, qualitatively different forms. We arrive, therefore, at the conclusion that these *most complex psychological formations arise from the lower by way of development.* (Vygotsky & Luria, 1994, p. 148)

Since this aspect is pivotal to understanding Vygotsky, Luriya [Luria] (1967) went on to give an explicit description of what Vygotsky actually meant:

> in tracing the early stages of ontogenesis, Vygotsky showed that the first steps in forming higher mental functions depend on more elementary processes that serve as a base. Complex concepts cannot be developed if there are insufficiently stable sensory perception and ideas; voluntary recall cannot be formed if there is not a stable substratum of immediate memory. However, in later stages of mental development the relationship between elementary and complex processes changes. Higher mental functions developing on a base of elementary mental processes begin to influence the base, and even the simplest forms of mental processes are reorganized under the influence of higher mental activity; it is enough to recall the part played by verbal classification in color perception to understand the full depths of this process. These facts compelled

Vygotsky to assume that the relationship between separate cortical zones changes during development, and if, initially, the formation of "higher" centers depends on the maturity of the "lower," ultimately the "higher" organize and influence the "lower" in fully formed behavior. (p. 57)

At this point the innatist *Fodor paradox* comes to play largely negating the role of the environment in the maturational role of development. This position is defined by Newman et al. (1989) in the following way:

Fodor (1980) points out the problem with the Piagetian constructivists position that arises when one attempts to derive a formal mathematical model of stage development: a higher order calculus or logic can derive lower order ones but cannot be derived from them; hence, it is very difficult to see how children can progress from "lower" logical stages to "higher" logical stages unless one posits (as Fodor would) that the "higher" stage is in some way innately in place and that what looks like constructivist stage development is in fact just the gradual maturation and environmental triggering of innate mechanisms. (p. 65)

On various occasions Fodor trys to reduce the logic of Vygotsky's position as being *innatist*. It is important to first state that Vygotsky was not opposed to a positioning of innate elements; indeed there is ample discussion of this aspect within biological materialism and the phylogenetic inquiry;[129] however, the discussion then proceeds to focus on culture when entering the realm of the higher mental capacities. Fodor's argument in general, is, however, wrong, providing its own contradiction:

He [Fodor] considers the "typical" concept learning experiment in which the subject is given a stack of cards of different colors and shapes and is asked to sort them into piles which might be labeled with a nonsense word such as "miv." The experimenter provides some materials, some interactions and differences in these conditions are studied to see what conditions promote, say, faster learning. Fodor claims that such work can develop information on [the] rate of learning and influences on learning ("fixation of belief') but cannot inform the investigator about where concepts come from, leaving inquires about "concept acquisition" to the nativist. But Fodor in fact tells us just where the concept comes from: *it comes from the experimenter.* There is a social origin for the concept, just as Vygotsky assumes. Of course in the case that Fodor uses ("miv" is red and square), the society which originates it is rather odd, small and restricted (the laboratory society) and the social interactions are rather dull and limited (the experimental procedure script), but nonetheless, the social origin is clear. (Newman et al., 1989, p. 66)

In 1985, Breiter updated the *Fodor paradox* with the inclusion of the problem of *internalization* that has been a reason for various cognitive scientists to dismiss the cultural-historical school altogether. Bereiter (cited in Newman et al., 1989) stated:

Following Vygotsky ... one might formulate the following explanation: Learning does, indeed depend on the prior existence of more complex structures, but these more

[129]cf. Newman et al. (1989, p. 66).

complex cognitive structures are situated in the culture, not the child. . . . Through
. . . shared activities the child internalizes the cognitive structures needed to carry on
independently. Such an explanation, satisfying as it may appear, does not eliminate the
learning paradox at all. The whole paradox hides in the word "internalizes." How does
internalization take place? (p. 67)

The problem of *internalization* is certainly a cogent example of trying to
make the innermost plane visible to observation. In reality one can only view the
processes involved by describing sequential patterning and since commensura-
bility will never be reached on this issue, it can always be used as a point for
rejecting further ideas of Vygotsky. The problem itself has been clearly explained
by Chris Sinha (1988), who stated the following: "if the individual cognitive
subject is seen as being an internalized product of social life and organization,
and not a product of biology, then what is the nature of the subject (or proto-
subject) which is initially responsible for the act(s) of internalization?" (p. 102).
Sinha then goes on to conclude that

such considerations lead to the conclusion that . . . the Vygotskian theory of internalization reproduces in its internal logic the very divisions . . . which it strives to overcome. . . . with the assumed layering of the socio-cultural over the biological stratum
a break in the biological does not happen, hence Vygotsky ultimately did not *break*
with behaviorism. . . . scientists are still struggling with the understanding of evolution in Darwinian terms, and it is also true that there was a belief in these theories by
many Russian scholars during the 1920s, with the question being posed: "is the biological core then biological only?" (p. 103)

Two points need to be made regarding Vygotsky's position: (1) he was interested in Darwin's theories and some say that he wanted to establish a phylogenetic model paralleling the biological one, although many Vygotskian experts
disagree with this understanding. However, Vygotsky's focus on human speech
was the differentiating factor within this argument, where human speech, with its
symbolic and representational functions, was never a part of the animal kingdom.
(2) Vygotsky wrote within the mode of a *metatheory* often using the essence of
previous psychological models to elaborate his own systematic approach. His
instrument of analysis, for the most part, was the use of dialectics, not focusing
solely on "thesis," nor on "antithesis," but on "synthesis," which is one of the
differences with Fodor. Vygotsky's aim was not to negate, nor even break away
from behaviorism, establishing a replacement for this concept. His aim was to
redirect the basic understanding of behaviorism, placing it within the lower
mental processes on which the higher mental processes were based, hence there
is an automatic reciprocity between the two. There was a fusion of individual and
biological with social and cultural, all of which was meant to form a holistic
understanding of human history. Perhaps the most important aspect in clarifying
the problem of *internalization* is to explain two points: (1) "From the principle
of mediation emanates the postulate that the structure of external and internal

activity constitutes a unity . . ." (Asmolov, 1986–87, p. 92); (2) ". . . the principle of mediation is inseparable from the principle of internalization" (Asmolov, 1986–87, p. 92). There are three basic aspects that need to be distinguished in comprehending the concept of "internalization," which begin with *individualization*, with this understanding relating to the *general genetic law of development*. The second area is *intimization*, which is the transition from "we" to "I" in child development. The third point is the *production of the internal "level of consciousness,"* where the external is not mechanically transformed into an equivalent internal aspect. Internalization is not a mechanical transfer, but a system of ontological transformations (cf. Asmolov, 1986–87, pp. 94–96). One of the main substrates underlying this understanding is the connection of the individual to the social, and the social to the individual, which forms a dialectic.

Newman et al. (1989, pp. 67–68) go on to explain the underlying problem of the *Fodor paradox* that revolves around the view of the individual as an autonomous functioning member of society, without a socialized setting to relate to. In order to better understand these two positions E. Watson (1995) stated that

> according to Fodor, it is sufficient for a semanticist to study the relationship between a single individual's mental representations and the objects in that single individual's mental representations and the objects in that single individual's environment. Fodor's position ignores both the social and the communicative dimensions of language. (p. 47)

The Vygotskian position is radically different, with the ingenious aspect of the *general genetic law of development* being placed within the Zone of Proximal Development, which is the reciprocal, dynamic, dialectical, asymmetrical, nonlinear approach to child (and many aspects of adult) development. Within Vygotsky's understanding there is a blending of individual and social, or of the innate and experiential within a framework of modeling by more capable peers or teachers. The end result is one of *self-regulation* and self-realization of one's dreams, goals, and so on. It is at this point that Peeter Tulviste's (1991, p. 30) statement becomes very important, with the question being raised as to whether natural–scientific explanations should be offered as tools of analysis within higher mental processes, since their origin is cultural–historical (within the Vygotskian understanding of these terms). The other question arises as to what the rationalist position offers in terms of explaining phenomenon such as "internalization," apart from stating that such a concept is innate, implying that it is beyond explanation. And without any definition or explanation of issues such as "internalization," what then does the *Fodor paradox* actually represent?

One of the problems stated by some cognitive scientists who reject Vygotsky has been the assumption that because there is not a primary focus on innatism within the cultural realms of higher psychological processes, then by way of elimination, it is automatically assumed that Vygtosky must have been a behaviorist. Caution is offered at this point, as well as an exact reading of Vygotsky, which will show a different interpretation of this conclusion. It appears that within much of the "objective" scientific approach, there is an automatic side taking, "either this side or the other," with little understanding left for the middle ground. Vygotsky's thoughts are a sincere attempt to explain higher mental processes within a functional approach, whereas assumptions such as the *Fodor paradox* offer no explanations apart from a simple negation of hypotheses. It is, however, important to try and bridge the middle ground and maintain dialogue with both sides. An example of this attempt was given by a cultural–historical theorist, Michael Cole (1996, pp. 198–208), who has presented a bridge that spans the middle-ground of assumptions going beyond the rationalist understanding of "yes–no." Cole begins by presenting the debate between Chomsky and Piaget regarding the question, which has been discussed under the *Fodor paradox*. Instead of believing that language is "constructed on the basis of previously developed sensorimotor schemata, Chomsky argued for the existence of what has come to be called a language module" (Cole, 1996, p. 198). The argument goes on to state that development of a particular linguistic structure is tantamount to viewing the development of other physical organs. Jerry Fodor then continued with this line of thought when he wrote *The Modularity of Mind* (1983). Some of his hypotheses are that psychological processes are domain specific, and these principles remain innately specified; the domains do not interact directly, and modules cannot be influenced by other parts of the mind that *have no access to their internal workings*.[130] Now, the modularity hypothesis maintains both a strong and a weak hypothesis. Michael Cole reviewed the weaker version and concluded that

> my own view is that the weaker form of modularity—as skeletal principles and starting point—can be usefully combined with notions of cultural mediation. Such a combination offers an attractive way to account for the intertwining of "natural" and "cultural" lines of development as part of a single process. (Cole, 1996, p. 199)

Cole then attempted to view the development of human language with the following questions in mind: "must language be acquired through a process of culturally mediated learning or constructive interaction like any other human cognitive capacity? Or is language a specialized, bounded domain (module) which needs only to be triggered to spring into action?" (Cole, 1996, p. 200). The basic answer implied is that cultural–historical theory can learn from the modular approach, "as in the case of the biological study of organogenesis, to specify the nature of the interactions from which the 'language organ' emerges" (Cole, 1996, p. 200). The hypothesis infers that scholars supporting modularity would surely agree that language couldn't be acquired in isolation; therefore, tenets of the socio–historical–activity approach can perhaps be beneficial. Now, although this

---

[130]cf. Cole (1996, pp. 198–199).

attempt at bridging such diverse positions sounds like a good idea and is welcomed theoretically, the argument Cole offered appears in the end to be a bricolage of compromise. The approach itself is perhaps a starting point of a mutual discussion where *intentional* listening can be situated, even when theorists have extremely divergent views. However, in this case, when such discussions are conducted with the exclusion of the Vygotskian genetic–developmental approach there is little assumption that fruitful results will ensue. As well, a mutual understanding of terms is necessary before such discussions can actually take place. For example, there would be little ground for agreement if one side of the argument is convinced that the human *mind* takes place only within the individual, with no need for a socialized context. The other side would then be convinced that the human *mind* is situated within a process driven understanding that the *social* affects the *individual*, and that internalization is the bridge to understanding the mind. However, this pessimistic conclusion should not preclude future discussions of an honest nature between Vygotskians and other cognitive scientists. Before entering into the realm of mutual discussions and listening, some preliminary thoughts need to be reviewed within the understanding of *relativity (+ thought and language), representationalism, and perception.*

Relativity (Representationalism and Perception)

Ellen Watson (1995, pp. 47–65) established a schematic approach to the differences between innatism vs. relativity by positioning three men together with Vygotsky serving the function as a bridge: Fodor–Vygotsky–Whorf. Representing the extreme innatist position on the left is Fodor, with Whorf representing the extreme relativistic position on the right. The major area of general misunderstanding involves the position of these three men on the topic of *mental representations*. Only Fodor and Vygotsky are viewed here, with Fodor accepting the theory of mind as containing mental representations rather than *expressions of natural language*. Within the modular conception of language paralleling any human organ, Fodor's computationalism uses the metaphor of the mind as a computer. He stated (1975) that "the only psychological models of cognition that seem even remotely plausible represent such processes as computational" (p. 27). The point is that computational machines must be endowed with an internal system capable of representing information to them in order to process information in the first place. Then it is suggested that humans process information in a similar way, which precludes an innate facility. This style of argument rests on the understanding of *propositional attitudes* resulting from the tenets of analytic philosophy.[131]

---

[131]cf. Watson (1995, pp. 48–49).

> Mental representations such as beliefs, desires and fears are called "propositional atti-
> tudes" because the sentences we use to ascribe them have a common structure: each
> state can be analysed as a different attitude of a subject to a proposition. For example,
> the sentence "John believes that he left the stove on" says that a subject *John* has the
> attitude of *belief* to the proposition that *he left the stove on*; the sentence "John fears
> that he left the stove on" says that the same subject holds a different attitude (fear) to
> the same proposition. In contrast, mental states such as pain or hunger do not repre-
> sent attitudes to propositions; the states in question are said to lack "propositional
> content". (E. Watson, 1995, p. 49)

Once again, Fodor does not believe in positing theories within models representing the external world when working within psychology, all of which is called *methodological solipsism* with the mental state of the subject in isolation being enough for study and observation. This position serves as a springboard to the question, *What is the role of language?* Is it to be studied in isolation, or not? Vygotsky believed that language serves two major functions: social contact (e.g., communication); and representation, with both functions being intertwined.[132] The aspect of representation is most important for *self-regulation*; for example, "language used to represent the means–end and interpersonal aspects of communicative interactions leads to the development of 'inner speech' and linguistically mediated motivation" (Wertsch, 1985a, p. 83). Within his philosophy of concept formation Vygotsky distinguished between *meaning* and *reference*, which was similar to Frege's distinction between *sense* and *reference*. Frege's example of *the evening star* and *the morning star* was used to differentiate between equivalence and generality, both referring to the planet Venus:

> The names have the same referent, but different "modes of presentation" or "senses"
> are associated with each name . . . Frege insisted that the sense of a sentence is deter-
> mined by the sense of the words that make it up, and that the sense of a word is its
> general capacity to determine the sense of sentences of which it is a part. Sense thus
> determines reference, but not vice versa (Wertsch, 1985a, pp. 83–84).

Vygotsky's attempt was to relate equivalence to generalization, with Lee (1985) stating that: "Vygotsky's developmental problem was to show how words embodied multiple levels of generality that gradually become differentiated as equivalencies among items at the same level of generality" (p. 84).

One of the basic problems in understanding the philosophy of representation today revolves around the following dichotomy:

> Representation . . . has a dual meaning in psychological theory. In the first place, it can
> refer to the signs or symbols which human beings produce and exchange. In the second
> place, it can refer to the knowledge and beliefs underlying sign-using and other behav-
> iors, and the structure and organization of such knowledge and beliefs. Representa-
> tion, then, is at once a semiotic and a cognitive category. (Sinha, 1988, p. xiii)

---

[132]Lee in Wertsch (1985a, p. 82).

Within the Vygotskian perspective this understanding will have a direct effect on the transition from lexical *meaning* to personal *sense*, as well as establishing a connection between *scientific* and *spontaneous* concept formation.

Fyodor–Vygotsky–Whorf (Continuation of the Innatist Discussion)

It can be assumed that for Fodor communicative practices and language in general do not impact thought, which automatically brings the discussion into the age-old debate on *language* vs. *thought*. At this point, Whorf enters the picture by privileging language over thought; however, he omitted the individualized contextual settings of individuals across linguistic communities. It should be remembered that Whorf was trained as an engineer and "had a hard-headed, mechanistic sense of causality and an impatient disregard for the metaphysical aspects of language" (Berthoff, 1988, p. 4). As mentioned earlier, there is often an inherent problem involved within the traditional mathematical–rationalistic stance, which resonates a "yes–no," "right–wrong" positioning. Now a second problem of inference occurs regarding the position of Vygotsky. A similar example given previously was the accusation that if Vygotsky did not believe in attributing innatist principles to the higher mental capacities, then he must be a behaviorist. The same problem now arises relating to relativism. If Vygotsky were not to share the innatist position of Fodor then it is sometimes assumed by his critics that he must be in favor of relativism, which is often represented in the works of Whorf. There is an important argument in refuting this assumption and that is the initial understanding that Whorf misinterpreted the writings and assumptions of his teacher, Sapir, who was immersed in European philosophy.

> Whorf did not understand Sapir's philosophy of language . . . because he did not have adequate or appropriate ideas to think *with*—those concepts which Richards (1955) calls our "speculative instruments." Whorf was not a philosopher; he had neither philosophical interests nor philosophical instruments to guide his inquiry . . . Differentiating Sapir from Whorf requires both rhetorical and logical analysis. It is my conviction that Whorf borrowed Sapir's language, thinking that by deploying it he could be faithful to the precepts of the scholar he admired, but that in the process he distorted the ideas which that language had served. (Berthoff, 1988, p. 2)

Regarding Whorf, many questions arise, such as, *What is relative to what? Are certain languages better than others?* Certainly, it has been suggested that the Sapir–Whorf hypothesis is in reality not a hypothesis at all, because it cannot be tested in any way. This places Whorfian relativity on the extreme point of a scale, where the opposite extreme (Fodorian innatism) suffers from the same objection. It has also been hypothesized that Whorfian relativity was simply

> the creation of John B. Carroll, who introduced it in his edition of the papers of Benjamin Lee Whorf . . . Carroll's contention is that Whorf's "linguistic relativity"

was derived from the theories of Edward Sapir, whose classes Whorf attended at Yale. With the Sapir–Whorf hypothesis, Carroll institutionalized Whorf's misconception of Sapir's argument about the role of language in thought and culture. (Berthoff, 1988, p. 1)

With all of these caveats in place, E. Watson (1995) argues that Vygotsky can be placed in the middle between Whorf and Fodor:

> Contemporary semanticists can look to the work of Vygotsky for a middle way between the approaches of Fodor and Whorf. Fodor is motivated by a theory about the mind and perception inherited from the empiricists and inspired by science and scientific inquiry. He argues that thoughts are the primary bearers of meaning, and that natural language gets its meaning because it expresses thoughts. Whorf believes that people's metaphysical pictures of the world come from their culture via the language they speak. He proposes that language is primary and that thought, mind, identity and worldview are shaped by it. Vygotsky takes both a scientific, empirical perspective and a socio-cultural one. He believes that language gets its nature as a meaningful sociocultural activity from the use to which individuals put it, and also that language shapes and transforms the mind of the individual who learns to use. The first major difference between Vygotsky and the writers above concerns his view of the reciprocal relationship between thought and language. (p. 58)

In backtracking somewhat, it has been stated that with the onset of Descartes' philosophy, mind and body were separate, implying that thought and language are also separate. Historically the debate regarding thought and language has taken various turns, with von Humboldt stating that thought is language and language is thought; Sapir believing that thought without language is impossible; Whorf claiming that language and thought are identical, and so forth. Vygotsky believed that thought and speech maintain different genetic origins, with thought having a prelinguistic root and speech having a pre-intellectual root, all of which intertwine via *engagements* and *separations* at the moment when speech takes on the same understanding as the use of tools in problem solving, somewhere around the age of two.

In 1972, Jerry Fodor wrote an overwhelmingly negative article on Vygotsky's philosophy, which basically missed the point of even capturing the essence of Vygotsky's theories. There were two responses to that article, one from H. Sinclair, who stated that "in his discussion of Vygotsky's well-known work on language and thought, Fodor appears to equate Piaget's views on cognitive development with those of Vygotsky's" (Sinclair, 1972, p. 317). The other response was from A. N. Leontiev & A. R. Luria, which also related to Vygotsky's position on thought and language:

> Dr. Fodor claims that Vygotsky's basic mistake lies in identifying language with speech, and thought with problem solving. His own idea is that the relation between the "deep structure" or "natural" or "inborn" language and the "superficial language codes" and their place in thought, has to be the central problem in cognitive psychology. At the same time, he assumes that the processes of thinking can have different

relations with speech and problem solving ("do we really solve a problem thinking 'Sunday will perhaps be warm?')". We quite agree that thinking can take many different forms and that speech is not at all identical to language . . . But we doubt that the theory of a "natural language" and "innate language codes" is valid . . . Thus any theory of a "natural" (ready made) or "innate" language seemed unacceptable to Vygotsky, and it remains unacceptable to both of us. It seems to us that a contrast between the immediate (natural) evolution of animal behavior and the social (or language-based) development of the human mind (of man's cognitive processes) has a much broader significance. This is why Vygotsky mentions the social origin of language and its influence on human thought as a central issue in scientific psychology . . . Vygotsky believed (as we do) that to think "Sunday will perhaps be warm" is impossible without the participation of language, not because Sunday is a verbal concept, but because any *conscious* thought of the future is a mental process which needs language as its base, and it is impossible to deal with the future (as with the past) without the aid of inner speech as a derivation of language. (Leontiev & Luria, 1972, pp. 312–313)

For Vygotsky, developed language competency requires problem solving, which then contains certain behaviors originating from a social setting. In understanding Vygotsky's ideas the role of "tool" is important as a bridge between thought and language/speech. "Vygotsky studied the use of tools both as a model for language use and as a psychological process in itself. Tools are significant for Vygotsky because he found that when human subjects begin to use them, language and thought begin to coalesce" (E. Watson, 1995, p. 60), all of which led to Vygotsky's understanding of *mediated activity*. Vygotsky was of the opinion that children bring innate qualities and natural motivations with them into mediated activity and interaction, thereby transforming them. This also includes a dynamism in human relationships, which allows for change and growth, where human beings can indeed transform objects, and as well, those objects in turn transform human beings.[133] In discussions on Vygotsky a resultant inflexibility sometimes arises, because tools are discussed as tools only. There are two important points here:

1. The tool is both an invention and possession of human beings for both individual and social use. In order to expand the understanding of tool, Michael Cole used the term "artifact" (Cole, 1996), which generates a broader field of discourse. As mentioned before, tools are equally important in creation of cultural activity, as well as in affording symbolic and representational value. In taking this understanding a step further, Michael Cole (1996) discussed artifacts so:

> According to the view presented here . . . an artifact is an aspect of the material world that has been modified over the history of its incorporation into goal-directed human action. . . . artifacts are simultaneously *ideal* (conceptual) and *material*. They are ideal in that their material form has been shaped by their participation in the interactions of

[133]cf. Watson (1988, p. 63).

which they were previously a part and which they mediate in the present. . . . the properties of artifacts apply with equal force whether one is considering language or the more usually noted forms of artifacts such as tables and knives that constitute material culture. . . . (p. 117)

Cole (1996, p. 121) then went on to use Mark Wartofsky's tripartite understanding of artifacts, with the first levels consisting *of primary artifacts*, such as axes, clubs, needles, and bowls. The second level consists of *representations of primary artifacts and of modes of action using primary artifacts*. These artifacts help *preserve* and *transmit models of action and belief*. Included are traditional beliefs, norms, constitutions, recipes, and so forth. The third level then consists of imagined worlds or *tertiary artifacts*, which are rules and conventions. This understanding of artifacts, according to Cole, is the *linchpin of cultural mediation*.

2.   The other point is that tools are implemented and needed for both human symbolic and representational purposes. In order to put these two lines of argument together, Sinha (1988) makes the point that

> . . . rather than seeing cultural evolution as "taking off" from . . . biological evolution, we should rather see evolutionary biological processes as having been . . . "captured" by an emergent cultural process, with ontogenetic processes . . . as a crucial catalyst and product of the co-evolution of culture and biology. . . . the emergence of human symbolic and representational capacities . . . is intimately connected with the emergence of cultural transmission and tool use . . . Tools are artefacts functioning as adaptive extensions of organismic movements . . . the structure of a tool may be seen as materially representative both of organismic structure . . . and of the local environment within which the tool functions. (pp. 104–105)

In returning to the comparison of Fodor–Vygotsky–Whorf, Wertsch (1991, pp. 43–45) lists three major differences between Whorf and Vygotsky: genetic analysis; the role of grammatical analysis. Vygotsky placed "word meaning" at the center of his analysis, whereas Sapir and Whorf "focused on the proposition or its linguistically encoded form, the sentence"; and language functions.

> According to Lucy (1987), "Whorf assumed that language was essentially referential in nature, that is, that it primarily fulfilled a referential function" (p. 125), an assumption that has inspired criticism and motivated several attempts to expand on these ideas by considering "functional," as well as "structural" relativity (Hymes, 1966; Ochs, 1988). In contrast, Vygotsky's notion of function and his claims about different functions played an essential role in his semiotic analysis. (Wertsch, 1991, p. 44)

Wertsch made the important observation that whereas Whorf was primarily concerned with linguistic analysis, Vygotsky was interested in psychological issues. In the end, we are still left without a definition of *innate* and what that actually means to psychology, to linguistics, and to other fields, such as SLA. Wilga Rivers (1983) offered suggestions by quoting different opinions:

Bruner says, "I am prepared to believe that in the linguistic domain the capacities for categorization and hierarchical organization are innate, and so, too, are predication, causation, and modification." Braine would accept as innate the mechanism that permits us to perceive temporal position and co-occurence relations. Ervin-Tripp observes that "order relations seem very apparent to children . . . Order is almost always accurately reproduced in imitations." Bever maintains that "there is not as much innate structure to language as we had thought, if the 'universal grammar' is stripped of those aspects that draw on other psychological systems" . . . (p. 91)

It is clear that any scholar, researcher, teacher, or person on the street, when referring to the higher mental processes, will in the end only be able to describe what he or she considers to be *innate* based on conjecture. This conjecture will, to a large degree, be based on thinking structured by the social environment and by perception.

Perception (Related to Innatism)

When relating the philosophical construct of innatism to the understanding of perception, the individual is automatically placed in a static position. By dividing the mind from the body, Descartes attempted to extract the role of perception from the "body." In beginning this discussion, it should be remembered that in accordance with Arnheim (1954), "perception does not start from particulars, secondarily processed into abstractions by the intellect, but from generalities" (p. 167). Here is a very old story relating to generalities and particulars:

We have all seen a box of Aunt Jemima Pancake Flour, with the picture of "Aunt Jemima" on the front. Dr. William Bridges of the New York Zoological Society has told this story about it: A United States planter in the Belgian Congo had some 250 natives working for him. One day the local chieftain called him and said he understood that the planter was eating natives, and that if he did not stop, the chief would order his men to stop work. The planter protested that he did not eat natives and called his cook as a witness. But the cook insisted that he did indeed eat natives, though he refused to say whether they were fried, boiled, stewed, or what not. Some weeks later the mystery was cleared up when the planter was visited by a friend from the Sudan who had had a similar experience. Between them they figured out the answer. Both had received shipments of canned goods from the United States. The cans usually bore labels with pictures of the contents, such as cherries, tomatoes, peaches, etc. So when the cooks saw labels with the picture of "Aunt Jemima," they believed that an Aunt Jemima must be inside! (Korzybski, 1951, pp. 185–186)

In returning to the philosophical discussion, Descartes placed perception in a curious position that remains ultimately algorithmic in nature. The present-day understanding of this term is reflected in computational thinking; for example:

The belief in the similarity of minds and computers . . . goes far beyond the belief that the behaviour of both is governed by rules and representations and that both are physical systems . . . for Descartes one of the ways of the acquisition of knowledge was deduction from clear and distinct ideas. To deduce, for Descartes, meant to infer from true and known principles by the step-by-step succession of elementary thoughts. . . . The rules of . . . cognitivists and computer scientists are based on the same principles . . . They are *algorithmic* . . . each step is dependent on the successful completion of the previous step. (Marková, 1982, p. 74)

This line of thought has been developed within both the Chomskyan and Fodorian model of linguistics. From the Vygotskian perspective it is important to distinguish the vastness of interpretation of perception. Just as *emotions* represent one of the bridges between the lower mental processes and the higher mental processes in Vvgotsky's thinking, the same is true for perception. It is surely a truism to view perception as being organized sensations, just as concepts can be viewed as organized perception. Going back to Hegel (not Descartes), everyday consciousness was established via perception, with the automatic assumption of mediated perception. Vygotsky put it this way:

The movement that previously had been the choice now serves only to fulfill the prepared operation. *The system of signs restructures the whole psychological process and enables the child to master her movement. It reconstructs the choice process on a totally new basis.* Movement detaches itself from direct perception and comes under the control of sign functions included in the choice response. This development represents a fundamental break with the natural history of behavior and initiates the transition from the primitive behavior of animals to the higher intellectual activities of humans. (Vygotsky, 1978, p. 35)

The consequences of an approach of not articulating and theorizing about semiotically mediated perception leads to some interesting conclusions, especially within mathematically rationalistic philosophy. The solipsist assumptions made by Fodor and others become confusing when comparing them to Vygotsky's psychology–philosophy. For Vygotsky, the understanding of *consciousness* presupposes the existence of another, simply because a person born and raised completely alone does not possess the understanding of *consciousness* within the framework of cultural history. Much of Western science and philosophy places ultimate value on "individualism" and on "the self," which is an epistemological issue of debate itself. Peter Steiner (1981), for example, went so far as to say that

western metaphysics would seem to be antisemiotic. The sign by definition violates the immediacy of self-presence. The essence of the sign is its otherness, for the sign is an entity that stands for another entity, that represents this other inevitably through spatial and temporal displacement. Suspicious of the sign, Western scholars have conceived of it in such a way as to obliterate its mediating quality. (p. 415)

In viewing Chomskyan linguistics from the point of view of perception, the quasi-scientific, mathematical stance turned at one point into a belief regarding the "holism" of the deep structure, without concomitantly describing elements of the deep structure. Even though the deep structure is no longer mentioned, it was not replaced within Chomskyan theory in its entirety. Within this understanding, perception, whether mediated or not, simply does not play a role in deriving truth values from descriptions of syntax alone, which leaves the individual situated as an autonomous human being within a static, nondevelopmental position. In refusing to accept a more precise definition of linguistic processes, within a perceptual framework, Chomskyan linguistics appears to claim an untenable position for any human being, that of infallibility. Indeed, with the inclusion of perception into linguistics, there is the automatic relativity infused into the theoretical construct, which admittedly contains distortions. At the same time, no human theory is devoid of such problems, since all human theories are devised by humans, who can only perceive in order to establish the theories in the first place. The problems resulting from the Gibson vs. Fodor, and Pylyshyn debate on perception is not included; however the relatively new understanding of perception ↔ environment within an ecoframework are producing results that will expand the Vygotskian dimension dramatically. In viewing perception from many areas there is today a connection that is often being made with the environment. Brunswik called it "ecological psychology," and Kurt Lewin many years ago referred to it as "psychological ecology." The connection being made is perhaps best described as the "life space" (Kurt Lewin) of each individual, which is a conscious field left open for each individual to create or establish his or her own reality, a space where personality development can take place, within a *boundary zone*. By *life space*, Lewin meant "the person and the psychological environment as it exists for him" (Lewin, 1943, p. 306). Another person relating perception to the environment is Urie Bronfenbrenner, who refers to ecological validity in research meaning that the real world must be reflected in research design, going beyond the non-natural setting of a clinic, a classroom, etc. Bronfenbrenner (1977, p. 35) lists three conditions necessary for ecological validity:

> (1) maintain the integrity of the real-life situations it is designed to investigate; (2) be faithful to the larger social and cultural contexts from which the subjects come; (3) be consistent with the participants' definition of the situation, by which he means that the experimental manipulations and outcomes must be "perceived by the participants in a manner consistent with the conceptual definitions explicit and implicit in the research design." (Cole, 1996, p. 226)

The short description of *perception* is a key element in questioning how human beings can believe in a linguistic theory devoid of perception in the first place. Without human perception there would not be a Chomskyan theory to discuss and *perceive*.

COMPETENCE (AND MENTAL REPRESENTATIONS)
(VYGOTSKIAN PERSPECTIVE)

Before beginning the Chomskyan *competence* issue from a Vygotskian perspective, the aspect of *constraints* is used in order to make a distinction. One of
the main problems within Chomskyan linguistics is the lack of constraints as a
result of the abstractness and opaque nature of the "ideal" construct being pro-
jected onto theory. Since Chomskyan linguistics views itself as being scientific,
it can then be stated that

> the art of scientific experimentation consists largely of arranging situations so the rele-
> vant constraints operate in this fashion. No doubt there are always other representations,
> unknown and perhaps for us unimaginable, that are also consistent with reality. The rep-
> resentations we present for falsification are limited by what we can imagine, which is to
> say, by the prevailing modes of representation within our culture, history, and species
> . . . We cannot see reality in it positively. We can only feel it through isomorphic con-
> straints operating upon competing local representations. (Hayles, 1993, p. 3)

Within this competition certain paradigms simply take hold, which meet
the needs of the collective and tend to be maintained for as long as they are
required. For example, as early as the 1960s, J. S. Bell proved mathematically
that subatomic particles are connected in a way that transcend time and space;
yet, Einstein's relativity theory still predominates in contemporary thinking,
which claims that it is impossible for a particle to travel faster than the speed of
light. Within the scientific orientation in the West it is interesting to see how
Euclidean geometry has continued to remain predominant even with the existence
of the non-Euclidean version discovered by N.I. Lobachersky. Therefore, the
acceptance of various theories within the scientific community is an interesting
phenomenon to be studied in its own right. Perhaps the most fascinating aspect
about Chomsky's linguistics is not his position on syntax or on grammar, but the
response, which the academic and general community lent in terms of supporting and popularizing this theory. It is remarkable that his theories have remained
viable for so long, because

> Chomsky's claim that his method was a scientific commonplace, though completely
> erroneous, was never challenged . . . An important consequence of this misstep was a
> correspondingly limited view of linguistics, the goal of which was now said by gen-
> erativists to be the construction of grammars. The limitations imposed by a starting
> point that took and ran with those things that looked like "clear cases" had now con-
> gealed into an extraordinarily limited view of the study of language itself
> . . . (J. Ellis, 1993, pp. 22–23).

In using Descartes' thinking as a model, Chomsky was then obliged to use
intuition (as opposed to *judgment*) as a basic parameter. Placing intuition and constraints within the same construct demands an initial definition that is not forth-

coming by Chomskyans. Constraints offer limitations on descriptions of reality, yet the most important aspect to remember is that constraints are the building blocks of an individual's sociohistorical–cultural reality. This automatically implies a sense of "constrained representation," which is culturally spatially specific. The example has been given of gravity, with Newton understanding this concept from the curvature of space. This view of perspectives can be extended *ad infinitum* to include many views on the laws of gravity, such as a Native American Indian understanding that "objects fall to earth because the spirit of Mother Earth calls out to kindred spirits in other bodies" (cf. Hayles, 1993, p. 30). Just as Newtonian physics might appear to some theorists to be as one-sided as the Native American Indian example, Hayles (1993) goes on to state that "no matter how gravity is conceived, no viable model could predict that when someone steps off a cliff on earth, she will remain suspended in midair" (p. 33). For Vygotsky, the system of constraints is present across the entire spectrum of his philosophy, but is especially transparent in his understanding of "tools": "tools therefore both *support* and *constrain*, via a material representational structure, adaptive organismic functioning, and, moreover, do so in the case of human societies within a cultural context of co-operative praxis and the division of labour" (Sinha, 1988, p. 105).

In returning to the realm of Chomskyan competence and its relation to the Vygotskian discussion, it can be stated that the attempt to explain competence without first understanding phylogeny, ontogeny, cultural history, and microgenesis from a genetic–developmental stance leaves *competence* as an area that cannot be defined, nor actually interpreted. In other words the mode of analysis of competence (in Chomskyan linguistics) must remain descriptive because the developmental stance is missing. At the same time, it is agreed that *intuition* is the guiding force in trying to answer many of the metaphysical problems arising in all four of Vygotsky's domains. For example, as has been mentioned, historians, archaeologists, and others are simply left with intuition in interpreting their findings, just as much as Chomksy is left with intuition in working within the model of competence.

> On the other hand, it is also possible to argue . . . that the Chomskyan approach, and by extension the majority of theories in Artificial Intelligence, constitute a logical terminus in the long process whereby representation has progressively been reduced to signification, and mind and mental process to the manipulation of formal (syntactically interpreted) symbolic entities. (Sinha, 1988, p. 25)

In extending this thought, Fodor with many of his caustic criticisms of so many models, has jettisoned "idea" or "representation" as being "isomorphic with both discourse and the world." Normally a representation must be a representation of something else. Now, propositional attitudes can be thought of as

relations of *commitment* (which include Fodor's criticisms), however, even these com-
mitments must be *discursively represented in order to have a pragmatic force*. And all
of this must be recognizable to an interpreter. With that in mind it then follows that
psychological concepts, as Vygotsky always emphasized, are signs, but they are not
copies, or surrogates, of discursive concepts, any more than discursive concepts are
surrogate "things." (Sinha, 1988, p. 72)

In viewing all four domains (i.e., phylogenetic, ontogenetic, sociocul-
tural/sociohistorical, and microgenetic) from a Vygotskian perspective, many
areas of explanation are forthcoming, such as the genetic–developmental line of
growth, categories including lower–higher mental processes (which will include
both innatist positions and areas of human autonomy that are relative), functionalism from the Russian perspective, perception, activity, history as change,
concept formation, inner speech, the general genetic law of development, tools,
artifacts, dialectic, monism, intuition–judgment, competence via self-regulation,
and symbolic meaning and representation, as well as many other areas. It appears
that in the end, the model of Chomskyan competence, which in reality does not
incorporate many of the afore-mentioned categories, is not a model but is itself
an *intuition*. Without real access to the construction of a model, *competence*
remains metaphysical. There are no laws derived from the competence structure
that will lead to a better understanding of developmental growth of human beings;
therefore, it remains static by nature, with the flexible component represented in
the additive–subtractive character that is incorporated in order to update its structuring in the first place. The major problem of the Chomskyan and Fodorian
approach to linguistics in general has been the following, stated by Chris Sinha
(1988):

Mental representations—cognitive signs—are necessary, to be sure, to the entertain-
ing of propositional attitudes: but they are secondary to, not the origin of, the discursive concepts actuated in natural language, which the subject must appropriate in order
to perform communicative acts. Cognitive development, in this theory, is the process
of appropriation of discursive concepts and positionings—and is a process open to
empirical study in precisely the way which Fodor's theory denies. (pp. 23, 74)

The following chapter enters the realm of universal grammar and Vygotskian understanding of grammar that is used in real language use.

5

Universal Grammar—SLA—Grammar from a Vygotskian Position

The Chomskyan revolution in linguistics took place during a time in history when there was a massive effort in the United States to rectify injustice and restore rights to the socially disadvantaged. The underlying linguistic philosophy Chomsky offered was the innateness each individual had in the *unfolding* of the mother tongue, which also implied an innate sense of equality. Chomsky did cause a real revolution and his theories are perhaps the most discussed linguistic theories around the world, all of which have lasted for almost half a century. Chomsky's primary aim was to establish a "holistic" framework for linguistics, beyond the S—R understanding of the times by philosophically placing *intuition* at a higher level than *reflexes*. This philosophy was admirable at that point in history; however, insurmountable problems have appeared within the practical components of *competence*. One problem which arises, from a Vygotskian perspective, is the following: "of further importance to the structural or descriptive linguist was the notion that language could be dismantled into small pieces or units and that these units could be described scientifically, contrasted, and added up again to form the whole" (Brown, 1987, p. 9). In viewing Chomskyan linguistics from the perspective of the contemporary world, it appears that linguistics is not hermetically sealed from political and economic events that influence world opinion, hence scientific opinion, all of which change over time. Indeed, the scope and direction linguistic theories will take in the future will reflect a conscious (and unconscious) need to establish acceptable parameters, all of which will be defined by collective needs. The traditional picture of the "ideal speaker–hearer" will soon be a part of history, not only as a result of new images being produced, but also because of a global shift in dominant populations, demonstrating that "for some years we have been witnessing the fall of the ideal speaker–hearer and the rise of the actual language use" (Coulmas, 1987, p. 139). Another contention has been the general understanding of grammar, which was so idealized and abstract that even Chomsky has been accused of not being grammatical. One example of this complexity is as follows:

> even the famous sentence through which Chomsky attempted to demonstrate that grammaticality was independent of meaningfulness ("colorless green ideas sleep furiously") should have shown just how wrong he was. This was . . . a plainly ungrammatical sentence, and for reasons that demonstrated again the link of grammar and semantics: the structure of the English noun phrase has a place for a color word, but only for one and this sentence had two. The grammar of the noun phrase cannot be described without reference to the position occupied by color words, which constitutes a semantic category *and* a grammatical one. (Ellis, 1993, p. 99)[134]

In moving from rules to parameters, the playing field in Chomskyan linguistics changed and became more diffuse in terms of "setting" boundaries where needed; and, at the same time there has not appeared to be an inclusion of topics that go beyond the "idealized speaker–hearer." In looking at some of the basic principles and parameters in Universal Grammar, the field remains limited with the majority of attention being directed at areas such as the following:

1. *The binding principle* (which constrains the *ways in which pronouns can relate to antecedents*: How "him" relates to "John" in "John likes him").
2. *The principle of subjacency*, which restricts *how far forms can be moved in the sentence*. "Which book did she say that Peter was reading?" is a grammatical sentence, but "What did she say that Joe told her Bill's guess that Pete liked" is ungrammatical, because "what" has crossed one "barrier" too many.
3. *The head parameter*, where complements precede or follow the heads *of phrases*.
4. *The pro-drop parameter*, whether the *subject of the sentence has to be actually present or not*; Spanish is pro-drop, English is not. For example, *va a la escuela*, with "va" meaning he, she, or you (formal). In English, these pronouns must be explicit.
5. *The opacity parameter*, whether negative elements and adverbs precede or follow the main verb; "John *often* drinks wine" versus French "Jean boit *souvent* du vin." (cf. Cook quoted in N. Ellis, 1994, pp. 478–479).

[134]Florian Coulmas presents a humorous quote on *idealized* grammar by Gertrud Stein: "Grammar is as disappointed not is a grammar is as disappointed. Grammar is not as grammar is as disappointed" (Coulmas, 1987, p. 139).

Apart from the obvious limitations within the range of topics analyzed, there is a further problem. In applying UG to SLA the question arises as to whether L2 learners even have access to UG, with some researchers saying "yes" (i.e., Felix, 1985; Flynn, 1983; Hilles, 1986; Mazurkewich, 1985; Tomaselli & Schwartz, 1990; White, 1988; Zobl, 1990), and some claiming "no" (i.e., Bley-Vroman, 1989; Clahsen & Muysken, 1986, Schachter, 1988).[135] If L2 learners do not have direct access to UG, can they reach grammatical correctness via their L1, and what does this mean? or,

> the argument here is that a choice has to be made between . . . metaphors, certainly so far as Second Language Acquisition is concerned. For the question of access is meaningless if UG is not in fact separate from the grammar itself; it would be bizarre to talk of the language faculty having, or not having, access to itself (Cook in R. Ellis, 1994: 495). It is stated that "if language learners do not have direct access to UG, they do through their knowledge of their L1" (Clahsen & Muysken, 1989). Another possibility is that L2 learners initially adopt L1 parameters to values inherent in the L2 . . . (Larsen-Freeman, 1991, pp. 324–325)

The concept of *values* can perhaps be used as a bridge between Chomskyan positions and the dialectical, cultural–historical position. In switching to the thoughts of Vygotsky it should first be stated that because the genetic–developmental aspect is not incorporated into UG theories, innatism/nativism does not allow for an *active* component with the individual partially being able to determine his/her own development. Therefore, without any dialectical stance little room is left for potential individual change, which automatically positions the learner in a passive situation where theory is not as effective as it could be. Therefore, Chomskyan theory cannot be compared to Vygotskian semiotics. As well, Rod Ellis (1994) has warned that "a UG-based theory, for example, is to be understood in terms of the field of Chomskyan linguistics from which it was developed, and needs to be evaluated with regard to the contributions that it makes to this field" (p. 685). In all fairness, if Chomsky stated that he would not recommend his linguistic theory for SLA pedagogy, then he should not be judged for having excluded these realms. Chomskyan SLA researchers need to present UG as a viable structure for SLA in general, and for the L2 classroom (and in L2 textbooks) where second language grammar is learned. With the failure of Krashen's attempt to apply Chomskyan principles to L2 acquisition–learning during the 1980s, it is not surprising that many SLA Chomskyan scholars have turned to research regarding theoretical language principles in general, avoiding necessary research applied to L2 pedagogy. At the same time, much interest is evolving in the area of cultural–historical principles.

---

[135]Examples listed in Larsen-Freeman (1991). The names listed are to be found in Larsen-Freeman's article, p. 324. Also, see Rod Ellis (1994, p. 443) *The study of second language acquisition.*

Vygotskian Grammar (L1 and L2)

There are three aspects of Vygotsky's psychology–philosophy of direct relevance to the principles of learning grammar (both first and second language), and to UG in general. First, Vygotsky felt that *grammar* serves as a mediating bridge between *scientific* and *spontaneous* concepts (cf. Lee in Wertsch, 1985a, p. 87), at which point the level of everyday knowledge would play a role. Many of the examples given in this section, relating to grammar, will refer to the acquisition of foreign languages, a topic Vygotsky discussed in his thoughts on grammar. It should not be forgotten that during Vygotsky's youth learning a foreign language was taught as a standard part of classical education, with literature, poetry, and theater being the focus of the content of the L2 studies. Vygotsky stated that

> if the development of the native language begins with free, spontaneous use of speech and is culminated in the conscious realization of linguistic forms and their mastery, then development of a foreign language begins with conscious realization of language and arbitrary command of it and culminates in spontaneous, free speech. But, between those opposing paths of development, there exists a mutual dependency just as between the development of scientific and spontaneous concepts. This kind of conscious and deliberate acquisition of a foreign language obviously depends on a known level of development of the native language . . . (John-Steiner, 1985, p. 350)

Second, within Vygotskian theory the study of grammar assumes two types of subjects, both a *grammatical* and a *psychological* subject. The example mentioned is that of a clock falling down with the emphasis on the possibility of a change of meaning, depending on the focus of the *subject*:

> Suppose I notice that the clock has stopped and ask how this happened. The answer is, "the clock fell." Grammatical and psychological subject coincide . . . But if I hear a crash in the next room and inquire what happened, and get the same answer, subject and predicate are psychologically reversed. I knew something had fallen—that is what we are talking about. "The clock" completes the idea. The sentence could be changed to "What has fallen is the clock"; then the grammatical and the psychological subjects would coincide. (Vygotsky, 1994a, p. 220)

Third, in viewing the learning of grammar there still remains the assumption that there is only one grammar, one syntax, and so on. Because grammar is used by children and adults unconsciously every day, it is often taught within the L2 classroom, for example, as if one must have privileged access to the grammatical structures themselves. The privileged position assumed could also be related to the privileged *ideal speaker–listener.* In the postmodern world of multivocal plurality, Vygotsky's understanding of grammar is most advanced and current for the classroom setting. Fourth, Vygotsky stated in different works that the syntax of grammar is internalized before the logic of grammar. He went on to say that *the grammar of thought is not the same in the two cases. One might even say that the syntax of inner speech is the exact opposite of the syntax of written speech, with oral speech standing in the middle* (Vygotsky, 1994a, p. 182). He continued, saying that

> grammar is a subject that seems to be of little practical use. . . . He conjugates and declines [sic] before he enters school. The opinion has even been voiced that school instruction of grammar could be dispensed with. . . . our analysis clearly showed the study of grammar to be of paramount importance for the mental development of the child . . . Grammar and writing help the child to rise to a higher level of speech development. . . . the development of the psychological foundations of instruction in basic subjects does not precede instruction, but unfolds in a continuous interaction with the contributions of instruction. (Vygotsky, 1994a, pp. 183–184)

In Vygotskian terminology grammar mediates between the upward growth of *spontaneous* concepts and the downward growth of *scientific* concepts (cf. Lee in Wertsch, 1985a, p. 87). For Vygotsky the bridge between the two is *grammar* and it is understood that *grammar* is dialectically positioned between spontaneous and scientific concepts. Vygotsky concluded with the thought that "the opinion has even been voiced that school instruction in grammar could be dispensed with. We can only reply that our analysis clearly showed the study of grammar to be of paramount importance for the mental development of the child" (Vygotsky, 1994a, p. 184).

In thinking about grammar more than a one-dimensional approach of dissection is necessary, with many levels converging. Heynick (1983) quoted Albert Einstein as stating that

> "if language is to lead at all to understanding, there must be rules concerning the relations between signs on the one hand, and on the other hand there must be a stable correspondence between signs and impressions." The rules referred to are grammatical, the relations are logical, the signs are lexical, and the impressions are, once again, those made upon the senses. (p. 55)

In order to teach or learn grammar, Belyayev (1964) was convinced that psychology must play a part in distinguishing the knowledge of grammar, as well as "the practical skills involved in using appropriate grammatical constructions in speech or writing" (p. 17). The first aspect will be *consciousness*, according to Belyayev, whereas the second aspect will require an automatic reaction and formation of linguistic response. What is important for the teacher is to have a clear understanding of *knowledge, acquired abilities, and habits.* At this point the teacher must be aware of concept formation, remembering that if the student does not have the appropriate concept behind the grammatical (or lexical) components, then repetition will be meaningless and unmotivated and will never result in internalization–appropriation.

In view of what has been stated concerning the multidimensionality of grammar, A. A. Leontiev (1973) offered some valuable thoughts on *functional grammar*, taking the discussion into the area of foreign language learning. He stated that "a model of the generation of verbal utterances is based on a rule for moving from a given 'content' to the various possible forms of its 'expression' in a particular language" (p. 22). In understanding the perspective Leontiev is implying one must first agree that for concept formation (here, grammatical concepts) to be formed there must be an initial motivation on the part of the learner. In beginning the analysis of a grammar placed within the functional parameters of the individual learner, a beginning point is the *speech act*, which automatically implies a psychological component with extralinguistic factors affecting different operational structures in various languages. Therefore, learning the direct object or accusative case indeed has a different psychological weight in different languages. In teaching traditional grammar, or L2 grammar from the UG point of view, there is often (but not always) a feel that subjacency, or the binding principle maintain a value equivalency that is then presented as isomorphic in all languages. Therefore, since grammar is known in the mother tongue, the net effect is that grammatical structures are the same across languages, substituting different lexems for the same content. With such an approach in place, it would be most difficult for a German speaker, for example, to learn Russian, where intrinsic differences are part and parcel of the accusative and dative grammatical forms. This leads to some basic problems in foreign language instruction:

> First, the problem of a functional grammar—that is, approaching language instruction from the standpoint of how to express a given content rather than from the standpoint of the significance of a particular formal means. And, second, there is the problem of differentiation of instruction in accordance with the various functions and types of speech. (Leontiev, 1973, p. 40)

In closing, it has been demonstrated that grammar is not totally an innate structure; indeed it is a dynamic process with many levels of psychological reality for both children and adults. Grammar is the anchor for bridging spontaneous with scientific concepts, and it serves a mediating role in personality development. Grammar, understood from a Vygotskian position, has a multidimensional character that offers new realms of understanding of the human psyche.

6

Conclusion

The attempt to polarize Chomskyan theories against Vygotskian theories, *inter alia*, is not totally necessary, but it seems to carry much energy for debate. Certainly there is equal validity to both areas, and within the pluralistic, multivocal postmodern framework of theory in general, a one-dimensional, monolithic approach seems out of date. Fieldwork linguistics, as well as homework linguistics or autonomous linguistics (Newmeyer, 1986, p. 12), psycholinguistics, sociolinguistics, and UG, should maintain equal validity. Researching nontemporal, nonhistorical phenomena is just as valid as researching specific criteria directly related to applicable results. However, one caveat is that if real time and real history are to be used within the matrix of research, then the understanding of nonlinear, asymmetrical movement must be recognized for any change to occur. As well, the ". . . traditional approach to science which attempts to understand the behavior of the whole by examining its parts piecemeal is inadequate for studying complex systems . . . Complex systems are also nonlinear" (Larsen-Freeman, 1997, p. 143). With that in mind, it is argued that there is one continuum of human language, although it has four varying positions: phylogeny, ontogeny, sociocultural history, and microgenesis. Within that continuum the paradox remains in that there is a modular systems approach, as well as an interrelated approach simultaneously, all of which we can only approximate within human cognition. We have no ultimate answers to the riddles of human language and we probably never will within third-dimensional existence. The approach here is to take traditional arguments that place Vygotsky and Chomsky in opposition to each other and point out the differences between the two. At the same time, there has been an attempt to demonstrate how consistent Vygotskian theory was over time although Vygotsky changed a couple of points within his theory as well (e.g., thoughts on consciousness). One can speak of a coherent Vygot-skian psychology–philosophy without resorting to certain periods of time.[136] This is not the case within Chomskyan linguistics where one needs to specify the model and time frame being used in order to discuss aspects such as Language Acquisition Device (LAD), competence, deep structure, and so on. At this point the ultimate paradox of the entire Chomskyan system is offered: Chomsky claimed from the beginning that language *springs forth* within innate qualities and does not develop through environmental factors, although he did allow for the theoretical construct of *pragmatic competence.* However, the following state-ment makes Chomsky's position clear: "But overall this discussion has found no way in which principles of UG are learnable from the environment" (Cook & Newson, 1996, p. 102). Regarding the minimalist approach, two points become clear: (1) Even within an innatist, computational model, the environment must be included into the research design in order to have a living, dynamic theory; and (2) Chomsky's approach has been one of *addition* and *subtraction*, with each new theory and phase being constructed and reconstructed from a relative stance, and not an innatist and deductive stance. Cook & Newson (1996) stated that "one important difference between minimalism and GB is that, in the former [mini-malism], structures are built up piecemeal" (p. 323). This must result in a reduc-tionist theory. And the final verdict is then offered by Cook & Newson (1996) as well: "However, given that the whole programme [minimalist] depends on the ability to reduce certain elements of the grammar to more basic elements and relations, the most important question is whether such reduction is possible" (pp. 326–327). At this point it is clear that the Chomskyan experiment has not been successful as a single and unified linguistic theory of language, even according to the standards set down by Chomsky himself.

At the same time, Vygotsky is held accountable for the holistic approach of his theories, just as Chomsky will be in future. Vygotsky's vision was holistic from the beginning, using a Humboldtian–Spinozian understanding of experi-mentation. Chomsky, on the other hand, actually claimed to begin from the holistic tenets of Descartes, to end up by establishing small, atomistic segments of a linguistic–grammatical theory, to continually discard earlier elements in a most non-innatist fashion. This build up effect automatically implies reduction-ist logic; however, it is virtually impossible to reduce Chomskyan theories back to the model of generative grammar. Any form of reductionism was one of the

---

[136]Certainly Vygotsky's overall career can be divided into various phases, but there is a logical con-sistency of his thoughts from 1917 until his death in 1934. An example of viewing the phases of Vygotsky's works have been given by Minick (1987, pp. 17–34) who divided Vygotsky's thought into three phases:

          1925–1930   Instrumental Phase
          1930–1932   Interfunctional Phase
          1932–1934   Semiotic Phase

major caveats given by Vygotsky regarding the crisis in psychology during the 1920s.

The closing statement might seem paradoxical and surprising to some, after establishing the lack of similarity between Chomsky and Vygotsky; however, in line with the new understanding of Chaos Theory and the hologram, "[if we] can include everything coherently and harmoniously in an overall whole that is undivided, unbroken, and without a border, then . . . from this will flow orderly action within the whole" (David Bohm quoted in Gergen, 1995, p. 239). The trick in this understanding, from a Vygotskian perspective, is to view the whole from the standpoint of "units of analysis" that does not attempt to break down the whole into its elements, reconstructuring it again; this under-standing functions together within the fluid, dynamic aspects of Vygotsky's thought within a higher, Spinozian structure. Some examples are as follows: dialectics within Spinozian monism, sense within meaning, concept development within periodization (e.g., stages of development), consciousness within the unconsciousness, and so forth. In other words, Vygotsky's understanding of the "whole" is a future-oriented approach that transcends any established scientific theory building to date.

Vygotsky was quite critical of the development of psychology during his lifetime. For example, he stated: "the fact is that because of the crisis in psy-chology, all concepts have become meaningless and vague. They change depend-ing on the investigator's point of view . . . in explaining lower forms of behavior we should use a principle that we usually use to explain higher forms of behav-ior, whereas, until now, psychologists have relied on principles used to explain primitive behavior to analyze a higher level" (Vygotsky, 1981, pp. 147, 152). The following quote is long and can be interpreted as a summary of Vygotsky's theoretical *essence* in his own words. In speaking of the three stages of the evolutionary stages in ontogeny, Vygotsky stated that

> instinct, or the innate, inherited fund of behavioral modes, forms the first stage. The second stage consists of what Bühler called the stage of training, or the stage of habits or conditioned reflexes, i.e., conditioned reflexes mastered and acquired in personal experience. Finally, and still higher, we have the third stage, the stage of intellect or intellectual responses that fulfill the function of adaptation to new conditions. In Thorndike's words, these constitute the organizing hierarchy of habit used for solving new problems . . . The old level does not die when a new one emerges, but is copied by the new one and dialectically negated by being transformed into it and existing in it. Instinct is not destroyed, but "copied" in conditioned reflexes as a function of the ancient brain, which is now to be found in the new one. Similarly, the conditioned reflex is copied in intellectual action, simultaneously existing and not existing in it. Two equally important problems confront science: it must be able to distinguish the lower stages in the higher, but it must also be able to reveal how the higher stages mature out of lower ones . . . The history of signs, however, brings us to a much more general law governing the development of behavior. Janet calls it the fundamental law of psychology. The essence of this law is that in the process of development, children

begin to use the same forms of behavior in relation to themselves that others initially used in relation to them . . . A sign is always originally a means used for social purposes, a means of influencing others, and only later becomes a means of influencing oneself . . . Any function in the child's cultural development appears twice, or on two planes. First it appears on the social plane, and then on the psychological plane. Thus, the child is the last to become conscious of his/her gesture . . . Above all, in the widest sense of the word . . . everything that is cultural is social . . . Further, one could point to the fact that the sign, like the tool, is separate from the individual and is in essence a social organ or a social means . . . On the basis of experiments we can say that the child—even the prodigy—can never master the last stage in the development of operations immediately or any earlier than by going through the first two states . . . It seems to me that it would be scientifically dangerous to restrict ourselves to two classes of development of a child's behavior, inherited and acquired experience . . . On the one hand, we have habits inherited for the adaptation to the more or less protracted conditions of individual existence. On the other hand, we have an entire hierarchy of habits directed at solving new problems as they confront the organism, in other words, the hierarchy of those responses about which we have been speaking. The connections among the developmental stages that interest us in child psychology are dialectic (Vygotsky, 1981, pp. 147–173).

Dimitry Leontiev, the son of A. A. Leontiev, and V. S. Sobkin, make a very eloquent statement in claiming that Vygotsky's views are a preparation for the twenty-first century.

Vygotsky treated human psychology not as a natural science but rather as a synthetic science, integrating natural, humanitarian, and social knowledge. That is why so many of Vygotsky's enlightening hypotheses and insights have not yet been realized in concrete research on and knowledge of the human being. Vygotsky moved toward a new psychology, but it is still new even for us in the 1990s. Perhaps it is the science of the human mind for the next century . . . The more time has passed since Vygotsky's death, the more we see him ahead of us, lighting our path (Sobkin & D. Leontiev, 1992, p. 192).

To add one other note in concluding these thoughts: Lev Kravtsov, the great grandson of Vygotsky, is of the opinion that it would be appropriate for future scholars interested in Vygotsky to not only analyze and dissect every word he wrote, but to adopt Vygotsky's vision of approaching problem solving from a holistic point of view, trying to view contemporary problems through the spirit and eyes of his great grandfather.[137] In closing, it seems appropriate to end in the way Vygotsky loved best. Dobkin (1982) remembers that "he [Vygotsky] even grew more fond of Tyuchev's poetry in those years. And with Tyutchev too he

---

[137]One of many private discussions with Lev G. Kravtsov during June 1999 in Moscow, Rostov-on-Don, Belaya Kalytva, Russia.

was able to find "his own" lines, which were not purely lyrical but had a philosophical message. He would often recite these lines:

> We still believe in miracles
> For all the lessons and the Truths
> That life has taught us;
> We know there's beauty that won't pall
> And strength that cannot be exhausted;
> That flowers of a loveliness unearthly
> To earthly withering will not succumb.
> And dewdrops, fallen on them in the morning,
> Will not be dried up by the midday sun.
> It is a faith that won't deceive you
> If you live by it alone from first to last;
> Not everything that flowered once must wilt,
> Not everything that was must pass. (p. 31)

References

Aidman, E. V., & Leontiev, D. A. (1991). From being motivated to motivating oneself: A Vygotskian perspective. *Studies in Soviet Thought, 41*, 137–151.

Akhutina, T. V. (1978). The role of inner speech in the construction of an utterance. *Soviet Psychology, XVI*, 3–30.

Alatis, J. E. (Ed.). (1993). *Georgetown Roundtable on Languages and Linguistics.* Washington D.C.: Georgetown University Press.

Arnheim, R. (1954). *Art and visual perception.* Berkeley: University of California Press.

Ash, M. G., & Woodward, W. R. (Eds.). (1987). *Psychology in twentieth-century thought and society.* Cambridge, England: Cambridge University Press.

Asmolov, A. G. (1986–87). Basic principles of a psychological analysis in the theory of activity, *Soviet Psychology, Winter*, 78–102.

Asmolov, A. G. (1998). *Vygotsky today: On the verge of non-classical psychology.* Commack, New York: Nova Science Publishers, Inc.

Au, K. H. (1992). Changes in a teacher's view of interactive comprehension instruction. In L. C. Moll (Ed.), *Vygotsky and education: Instructional implications and applications of sociohistorical psychology* (pp. 271–286). Cambridge, England: Cambridge University Press.

Babcock, B. (1980). Reflexivity: Definitions and discriminations. *Semiotica, 30*, 14.

Bailey, R. W., Matejka, L., & Steiner, P. (1978 [1980]). *The sign: Semiotics around the world.* Ann Arbor: Michigan Slavic Publications.

Bain, B. (Ed.). (1983). *The sociogenesis of language and human conduct.* New York: Plenum Press.

Bakhtin, M. (1981). *The dialogic imagination: Four essays by M. M. Bakhtin.* M. Holquist (Ed.), trans. C. Emerson and M. Holquist. Austin: University of Texas Press.

Bakhtin, M. (1984). *Problems of Dostoevsky's poetics.* trans. and ed. by C. Emerson Minneapolis: University of Minnesota Press; Manchester: Manchester University Press.

Bakhurst, D. (1986). Thought, speech and the genesis of meaning: On the 50th anniversary of Vygotsky's Myšlenie I Rec. *Studies in Soviet Thought, 31*, 103–129.

Bakhurst, D. (1991). *Consciousness and revolution in Soviet philosophy.* Cambridge, England: Cambridge University Press.

Bakhurst, D. (1996). Social memory in Soviet thought. In H. Daniels (Ed.), *An introduction to Vygotsky* (pp. 196–218). London: Routledge.

127

Bakhurst, D., & Sypnowich, C. (Eds.). (1995). *The social self.* London: Sage Publications.

Bartsch, R., & Vennemann, T. (Eds.). (1975). *Linguistics and neighboring disciplines.* Amsterdam: North-Holland Publishing Company.

Basilius, H. (1952). Neo-Humboldtian ethnolinguistics. *Word, 8,* 95–105.

Bauer, R. A. (1959). *The new man in Soviet psychology.* Cambridge, Mass.: Harvard University Press.

Belyayev, B. V. (1964). *The psychology of teaching foreign languages.* trans. R. F. Hingley. New York: MacMillan Company.

Berkhin, N. B. (1988). The problem of communication in K. S. Stanislavsky's works. *Soviet Psychology, XXVI,* 3.

Berthoff, A. E. (1988). Whorf and Sapir. *Semiotica, 71,* 1–47.

Bickhard, M. H., & Richie, D. M. (1983). *On the nature of representation: A case study of James Gibson's theory of perception.* New York: Praeger Special Studies.

Blake, R. R., & Ramsey, G. V. (Eds.). (1951). *Perception: An approach to personality.* New York: The Ronald Press.

Blanck, G. (1992). Vygotsky: The man and his cause. In L. C. Moll (Ed.), *Vygotsky and education: Instructional implications and applications to sociohistorical psychology.* Cambridge, England: Cambridge University Press.

Bohm, D. (1981). *The implicate order.* London: Routledge & Kegan Paul.

Botha, R. P. (1989). *Challenging Chomsky: The generative garden game.* London: Basil Blackwell.

Bronckart, J.-P. (1995). Theories of action, speech, natural language, and discourse. In J. V. Wertsch et al. (Eds.), *Sociocultural studies of mind* (pp. 75–94). Cambridge, England: Cambridge University Press.

Bronfenbrenner, U. (1979). *The ecology of human development.* Cambridge, Mass.: Harvard University Press.

Brown, D. (1987). *Principles of language learning and teaching.* Englewood Cliffs, NJ.: Prentice-Hall.

Brown, D. (1993). *After method: Toward a principled strategies approach to language teaching.* In J. E. Alatis (Ed.), *Georgetown roundtable on languages and linguistics.* Washington D.C.: Georgetown University Press.

Brown, R. L. (1967). *Wilhelm von Humboldt's conception of linguistic relativity.* The Hague: Mouton.

Brugger, W. (1972). *Philosophical dictionary.* trans. K. Baker (Ed.). Spokane, WA: Gonzaga University Press.

Bruner, J. (1974–75). From communication to language—A psychological perspective. *Cognition, 3,* 255–287.

Bruner, J. (1985). Vygotsky: A historical and conceptual perspective. In J. V. Wertsch (Ed.), *Culture, communication, and cognition: Vygotskian perspectives* (pp. 21–34). Cambridge, England: Cambridge University Press.

Bruner, J. (1987). Prologue to the English edition. In R. Rieber (Ed.), *The collected works of L. S. Vygotsky. Vol. 4: The history of the development of higher mental functions* (pp. 1–16). New York: Plenum Press.

Bruner, J. (1995). Meaning and self in cultural perspective. In D. Bakhurst and C. Sypnowich. (Eds.), *The social self.* London: Sage Publications.

Brunswik, E. (1943). Organismic achievement and environmental probability. *Psychological Review, 50,* 255–272.

Burgess, T. (1993). Reading Vygotsky. In H. Daniels (Ed.), *Charting the agenda: Educational activity after Vygotsky* (pp. 1–29). London: Routledge.

Cazden, C. (1972). *Child language and education.* New York: Holt, Rinehart, and Winston.

Chomsky, N. (1961). On the goals of linguistic theory. In S. Saporta (Ed.), *Psycholinguistics: A book of readings* (pp. 37–44). New York: Holt, Rinehart and Winston.

Chomsky, N. (1965). *Aspects of the theory of syntax.* Cambridge, Mass.: M.I.T. Press.

Chomsky, N. (1966). *Cartesian linguistics*. New York: Harper & Row.

Chomsky, N. (1972). *Language and mind*. Enlarged edition. New York: Harcourt Brace Jovanovich, Inc.

Chomsky, N. (1986). *Barriers*. Cambridge, Mass.: M.I.T. Press.

Chomsky, N. (1992). Explaining language use. *Philosophical Topics, 20*, Spring.

Chomsky, N. (1993a). A minimalist program for linguistic theory. In A. Kasher (Ed.), *The Chomskyan turn* (pp. 26–53). Oxford and Cambridge, Mass.: Basil Blackwell.

Chomsky, N. (1993b). *Language and thought*. Wakefield, RI: Moyer Bell.

Chomsky, N. (1996). *The minimalist program*. Cambridge, Mass.: The MIT Press.

Christophersen, P. (1973). *Second language learning: Myth & reality*. London: Penguin.

Cole, M. (Ed.). (1995a). *From Moscow to the fifth dimension: An exploration in romantic science*. Worcester, Mass.: Clark University Press.

Cole, M. (1995b). Socio-cultural–historical psychology: Some general remarks and a proposal for a new kind of cultural–genetic methodology. In J. V. Wertsch et al. (Eds.), *Sociocultural studies of mind* (pp. 187–214). Cambridge, England: Cambridge University Press.

Cole, M. (1996). *Cultural psychology: A once and future discipline*. Cambridge, Mass.: The Belknap Press of Harvard University Press.

Cole, M., & Scribner, S. (1974). *Culture and thought: A psychological introduction*. New York: John Wiley & Sons.

Cook, V. (1992). Evidence for multicompetence. *Language Learning, 42*, 4.

Cook, V., & Newson, M. (1996). *Chomsky's universal grammar: An introduction*. (2nd ed.). London: Basil Blackwell.

Coulmas, F. (1987). Kinds of production. In H. W. Dechert & M. Raupach (Eds.), *Psycholinguistics models of production*. Norwood, N.J.: Ablex Publishing Corporation.

Cupchik, G. C., & Laszlo, J. (Eds.). (1992). *Emerging visions of the aesthetic process: Psychology, semiology, and philosophy*. Cambridge, England: Cambridge University Press.

D'Agostino, F. (1986). *Chomsky's system of ideas*. Oxford: Clarendon Press.

Daniels, H. (Ed.). (1993a). *Charting the agenda: Educational activity after Vygotsky*. London: Routledge.

Daniels, H. (1993b). The individual and the organization. In H. Daniels (Ed.), *Charting the agenda: Educational activity after Vygotsky*. London: Routledge.

Daniels, H. (Ed.). (1996). *An introduction to Vygotsky*. London: Routledge.

Davydov, V. V. (1981). The category of activity and mental reflection in the theory of A. N. Leont'ev. *Soviet Psychology, XIX*, 3–29.

Davydov, V. V., & Markova, A. K. (1982–83). A concept of educational activity for schoolchildren. *Soviet Psychology, 21*, 50–76.

Davydov, V. V., & Radzikhovskii, L. A. (1985). Vygotsky's theory and the activity-oriented approach in psychology. In J. V. Wertsch (Ed.), *Culture, communication, and cognition* (pp. 35–65). Cambridge, England: Cambridge University Press.

Davydov, V. V., & Zinchenko, V. P. (1981). The principle of development in psychology. *Soviet Psychology, 12*, 22–46.

Davydov, V. V., & Zinchenko, V. P. (1989). Vygotsky's contribution to the development of psychology. *Soviet Psychology, 27*, 22–36.

Davydov, V. V., & Zinchenko, V. P. (1993). Vygotsky's contribution to the development of psychology. In H. Daniels (Ed.), *Charting the agenda: Educational activity after Vygotsky* (pp. 93–106). London: Routledge.

Davydov, V. V., Zinchenko, V. P., & Talyzina, N. F. (1983). The problem of activity in the works of A. N. Leontiev. *Soviet Psychology, 21*, 31–42.

Dechert, H. W., & Raupach, M. (Eds.). (1987). *Psycholinguistic models of production*. Norwood, N.J.: Ablex Publishing Corporation.

Deleuze, G. (1981). *Spinoza: Practical philosophy.* trans. R. Hurley. San Francisco: City Lights Books.

Díaz, R. M., Neal, C. J., & Amaya-Williams, M. (1992). The social origins of self-regulation. In L. Moll (Ed.), *Vygotsky and education: Instructional implications and applications of sociohistorical psychology* (pp. 127–154). Cambridge, England: Cambridge University Press.

Dobkin, S. (1982). Ages and days. In K. Levitin (Ed. V. V. Davydov), *One is not born a personality* (pp. 18–38). Moscow: Progress Publishers.

Eagle, H. (1978). Eisenstein as a semiotician of the cinema. In R. W. Bailey et al. (Eds.), *The sign: Semiotics around the world* (pp. 173–193). Ann Arbor: Michigan Slavic Publications.

Edinger, E. F. (1984). *The creation of consciousness: Jung's myth for modern man.* Toronto: Inner City Books.

El'konin, D. B. (1967). The problem of instruction and development in the works of L. S. Vygotsky. *Soviet Psychology, 5(3),* 34–41.

Ellis, J. M. (1993). *Language, thought, and logic.* Evanston, Ill.: Northwestern University Press.

Emerson, C. (1983). The outer word and inner speech: Bakhtin, Vygotsky, and the internalization of language. *Critical Inquiry, 10,* 245–264.

Emerson, C. (Ed.). (1984). *Problems of Dostoevsky's poetics.* trans. C. Emerson. Minneapolis: University of Minnesota Press; Manchester: Manchester University Press.

Emerson, C. (1996). Bakhtin, Vygotsky—The internalization of language. In H. Daniels (Ed.), *An introduction to Vygotsky* (pp. 123–142). London: Routledge.

Engels, F. (1925). *Dialectics of nature.* London: Lawrence and Wishart.

Felix, S. (1981). The effect of formal instruction on second language acquisition. *Language Learning, 31.*

Flavell, J. H., & Draguns, J. (1957). A microgenetic approach to perception and thought. *Psychological Bulletin, 54,* 197–217.

Florenskaya, T. A. (1989). Psychological problems of dialogue in light of the ideas of M. M. Bakhtin and A. A. Ukhtomskii. *Soviet Psychology, 27,* 29–40.

Fodor, J. (1972). Some reflections of L. S. Vygotsky's thought and language. *Cognition, 1,* 83–93.

Fodor, J. (1975). *The language of thought.* Cambridge, Mass.: Harvard University Press.

Fodor, J. (1981). *Representations: Philosophical essays on the foundations of cognitive science.* Cambridge, Mass.: M.I.T. Press.

Fodor, J. (1983). *Modularity of Mind.* Cambridge, Mass.: M.I.T. Press.

Gergen, K. J. (1995). Social construction and the educational process. In L. P. Steffe et al. (Eds.), *Constructivism in education.* Hillsdale, N.J.: Lawrence Erlbaum Associates.

Gray, J. A. (1966). Attention, consciousness and voluntary control of behaviour in Soviet psychology: Philosophical roots and research branches. In N. O'Conner (Ed.), *Present-day Russian psychology.* Oxford: Pergamon Press.

Habermas, J. (1987). *The philosophical discourse of modernity.* trans. F. Lawrence. Cambridge, Mass.: M.I.T. Press.

Haenen, J. (1995). Report of the Vygotsky conference, Moscow, September (1994). *Educational Psychologist, 30,* 103–104.

Haenen, J. (1996). *Piotr Gal'perin.* Commack New York: Nova Science Publishers.

Hall, J. K. (1995). (Re)creating our worlds with words: A sociohistorical perspective of face-to-face interaction. *Applied Linguistics, 16,* 206–229.

Harris, E. E. (1992). *Spinoza's philosophy: An outline.* New Jersey and London: Humanities Press.

Harris, R. A. (1993). *The linguistic wars.* New York and Oxford: Oxford University Press.

Hatch, E., Shirai, Y., & Fantuzz, C. (1990). The need for an integrated theory: Connecting modules. *TESOL Quarterly, 24,* 697–716.

Hayles, K. N. (1993). Constrained constructivism: Locating scientific inquiry in the theater of representation. In G. Levine (Ed.), *Realism and representation.* Madison: The University of Wisconsin Press.

Heynick, F. (1983). From Einstein to Whorf: Space, time, matter, and reference frames in physical and linguistic relativity. *Semiotica, 45,* 35–64.

Hickman, M. (Ed.). (1987). *Social and functional approaches to language and thought.* Orlando, FL: Academic Press.

Hjelmslev, L. (1943). *Prolegomena to a theory of language.* Madison: University of Wisconsin Press.

Holzman, L., & Newman, F. (1987). Thought and language about history. In M. Hickman (Ed.), *Social and functional approaches to language and thought.* Orlando, FL: Academic Press.

Hook, S. (Ed.). (1969). *Language and philosophy: A symposium.* New York: New York University Press.

Hoppál, M. (1987). Proxemic patterns, social structures, and world view. *Semiotica, 65,* 225–247.

Innis, R. E. (1982). *Karl Bühler: Semiotic foundations of language theory.* New York: Plenum Press.

Innis, R. E. (Ed.). (1985). *Semiotics: An introductory anthology.* Bloomington; Indiana University Press.

Innis, R. E. (1994). *Consciousness and the play of signs.* Bloomington: Indiana University Press.

Israel, J. (1979). *The language of dialectics and the dialectics of language.* London: Harvester Press.

Jaensch, E. R. (1930). *Eidetic imagery.* trans. O. Oeser. London: Kegan Paul, Trench, Trubner & Co. LTD.

Jakobson, R., & Pomorska, K (1983). *Dialogues.* Cambridge, Mass.: M.I.T. Press.

Janet, P. (1929). *L'évolution psychologique de la personnalité.* (The evolution of the psychology of personality). Paris: A. Chahine.

John-Steiner, V. (1985). The road to competence in an alien land: A Vygotskian perspective on bilingualism. In J. V. Wertsch (Ed.), *Culture, communication, and cognition.* Cambridge, England: Cambridge University Press.

Joravsky, D. (1987). L. S. Vygotskii: The muffled deity of Soviet psychology. In Ash et al. (Eds.), *Psychology in twentieth-century thought and society* (pp. 189–211). Cambridge, England: Cambridge University Press.

Karcevskij, S. (1929). Du dualisme asymétrique du signe linguistique. *Mélanges linguistique. Dédiés au Premier Congrès des Philologues Slaves.* Prague. Reprinted in Nedeln, Liechtenstein: Kraus-Thomson Organization Limited.

Karcevskij, S. (1982). The asymmetric dualism of the linguistic sign In P. Steiner (Ed.), *The Prague School: Selected writings, 1929–1946.* Austin: University of Texas Press.

Karpov, Y. V., & Bransford, J. D. (1995). L. S. Vygotsky and the doctrine of empirical and theoretical learning. *Educational Psychologist, 30(2),* 61–66.

Kharitonov, A. N. (1991a). Aspects of A. A. Potebnya's linguistic model and certain problems of verbal communication. *Soviet Psychology, 29,* 6–20.

Kharitonov, A. N. (1991b). Remediation as an aspect of understanding in dialogue. *Soviet Psychology, 29,* 6–21.

Koltsova, V. A. (Ed.). (1996). *Post-Soviet perspectives on Russian Psychology.* Westport, CT: Greenwood Press.

Korzybski, A. (1951). The role of language in the perceptual processes. In R. R. Blake & G. V. Ramsey (Eds.), *Perception: An approach to personality.* New York: The Ronald Press.

Kozulin, A. (1984). *Psychology in utopia: Toward a social history of Soviet psychology.* Cambridge, MA: M.I.T. Press.

Kozulin, A. (1986). The concept of activity in Soviet psychology. *American Psychologist, 41,* 264–274.

Kozulin, A. (1990). *Vygotsky's psychology: A biography of ideas.* New York: Harvester-Wheatsheaf.

Kozulin, A. (Ed.). (1994). *Language and thought.* Cambridge, MA: M.I.T. Press.

Kozulin, A., & Z. Presseisen, B. (1995). Mediated learning experience and psychological tools: Vygotsky's and Feuerstein's perspectives in a study of student learning. *Educational Psychologist, 30,* 67–75.

Larsen-Freeman, D. (1991). Second language acquisition research: Staking out the territory. *TESOL Quarterly, 25,* 315–350.

Larsen-Freeman, D. (1997). Chaos/complexity science and second language acquisition, *18,* 141–165.

Lee, B. (1987). Recontextualizing Vygotsky. In M. Hickman (Ed.), *Social and functional approaches to language and thought.* Orlando, FL: Academic Press.

Leiber, J. (1975). *Noam Chomsky: A philosophic overview.* Boston: Twayne Publishers.

Leont'yev, A. A. (1968–69). Inner speech and the processes of grammatical generation of utterances. *Soviet Psychology, VII,* 11–16.

Leont'ev, A. A. (1970). *Aktual'nye problemy psikhologii rechi i psikhologii obuchenia yazyku.* (Actual problems in the psychology of speech and of the psychology of education regarding language). Moscow: Moscow University Press.

Leont'ev, A. A. (1971). *Sprache—Sprechen—Sprechtätigkeit.* (Language—Speech—Speech ACtivity). trans. from Russian into German by C. Heeschen and W. Stölting. Stuttgart, Germany: Verlag W. Kohlhammer.

Leont'ev, A. A. (1973). Some problems in learning Russian as a foreign language (essays on psycholinguistics). Special issue of *Soviet Psychology, XI,* 1–103.

Leont'ev, A. A. (1976). Sense as a psychological concept. In J. Průcha (Ed.), *Soviet studies in language and language behavior* (pp. 90–91). Amsterdam: North-Holland Publishing Company.

Leont'ev, A. N. (1978). *Activity, consciousness, and personality.* Englewood Cliffs, NJ: Prentice-Hall.

Leontiev, A. A. (1978). The psycholinguistic aspect of linguistic meaning. In J. V. Wertsch (Ed.), *Recent trends in Soviet psycholinguistics.* Armonk, NY: M.E. Sharpe.

Leont'ev, A. A. (1981). Sign and activity. In J. V. Wertsch (Ed.), *The concept of activity* (pp. 241–255). Armonk, NY: M.E. Sharp.

Leont'ev, A. A. (1984). The productive career of Aleksei Nikolaevich Leont'ev. *Soviet Psychology, XXIII,* 6–56.

Leontiev, A. N. (1972). The problem of activity in psychology. *Soviet Psychology, 9,* 19.

Leontiev, A. N. (1981). *Problems of the development of the mind.* Moscow: Progress Publishers.

Leontiev, A. N., & Luria, A. R. (1972). Some notes concerning Dr. Fodor's' reflections on L. S. Vygotsky's thought and language. *Cognition, 1,* 311–316.

Leontyev, A. A. (1992). Ecce Homo: Methodological problems of the activity–theoretical approach. *Multidisciplinary Newsletter for Activity Theory, 11,* 41–45.

Leuninger, H. (1975). Linguistics and psychology. In R. Bartsch et al. (Eds), *Linguistics and neighboring disciplines* (193–207). Amsterdam: North-Holland Publishing Company.

Levine, G. (1993). *Realism and representation.* Madison: The University of Wisconsin Press.

Levine, N. (1984). *Dialogue within the dialectic.* London: George Allen & Unwin.

Levitin, K. (1982). *One is not born a personality: Profiles of Soviet education psychologists.* V. V. Davydov (Ed.). Moscow: Progress Publishers.

Lewin, K. (1943). Defining the "field at a given time." *Psychological Review, 50,* 292–310.

Luria, A. R. (1928). Psychology in Russia. *Journal of Genetic Psychology, 35,* 347–349.

Luria, A. R. (1974–75). Scientific perspectives and philosophical dead ends in modern linguistics. *Cognition, 3,* 377–385.

Luria, A. R. (1976). A neuropsychological analysis of speech communication. In J. Průcha (Ed.), *Soviet studies in language and language behavior.* Amsterdam: North-Holland Publishing Company.

Luria, A. R. (1979). *The making of mind.* M. Cole and S. Cole (Eds.), Cambridge, MA: Harvard University Press.

Luria, A. R. (1981). *Language and cognition.* New York: John Wiley & Sons.

Luriya, A. R. (1967). L. S. Vygotsky and the problem of functional localization. *Soviet Psychology.* Spring, *V*, 53–57.

Lyotard, J.-F. (1984). *The postmodern condition: A report on knowledge.* trans. G. Bennington & B. Massumi. Minneapolis: University of Minnesota Press.

Mamardashvili, M. K. (1990). The problem of consciousness and the philosopher's calling. *Soviet Psychology, 29*, 6–26.

Marková, I. (1982). *Paradigms, thought, and language.* New York: John Wiley & Sons.

Marková, I., & Foppa, K. (Eds.). (1990). *The dynamics of dialogue.* New York: Harvester-Wheatsheaf.

Matejka, L. (1978) [1980]. The roots of Russian semiotics of art. In R. W. Bailey et al. (Eds.), *The sign: Semiotics around the world.* Ann Arbor, Michigan Slavic Publications.

Matejka, L. (Ed.). (1978). *Sound, sign and meaning: Quinquagenary of the Prague Linguistic Circle.* Ann Arbor: University of Michigan Press.

McCarthy, D. A. (1929a). Note of the vocal sounds of a blind–deaf girl. *Journal of Genetic Psychology, 36*, 482–484.

McCarthy, D. A. (1929b). A comparison of children's language in different situation[s] and its relation to personality traits. *Journal of Genetic Psychology, 36*, 583–591.

McCarthy, D. A. (1930). The language development of the preschool child. Minneapolis: The University of Minnesota Press.

Minick, N. J. (1996). The development of Vygotsky's thought. In H. Daniels (Ed.), *An introduction to Vygotsky* (pp. 28–52). London: Routledge.

Minick, N. (1987). The development of Vygotsky's thought: An introduction. In R. Rieber (Ed.), *The collected works of L. S. Vygotsky. Vol 3: Problems of the theory and history of psychology* (pp. 17–36). New York: Plenum Press.

Modgil, S., & Modgil, C. (Eds.). (1987). Noam Chomsky: Consensus and controversy. New York: The Falmer Press.

Moll, L. C. (Ed.). (1992). Vygotsky and education: Instructional implications and applications of sociohistorical psychology. Cambridge, England: Cambridge University Press.

Moore, R., & Carling, C. (1987). Chomsky: Consensus and controversy—Introduction. In S. Modgil et al. (Eds.), *Noam Chomsky: Consensus and controversy* (pp. 11–28). New York: The Falmer Press.

Morson, G. S. (1983). Who speaks for Bakhtin?: A dialogic introduction. *Critical Inquiry, 10*(2), 225–244.

N. A. (1983). *A tribute to Roman Jakobson, 1896–1982.* Berlin, New York: Mouton.

Newman, F., & Holzman, L. (1993). *Lev Vygotsky: Revolutionary scientist.* London: Routledge.

Newman, D., Griffen, P., & Cole, M. (1989). *The construction zone: Working for cognitive change in school.* Cambridge, MA: Cambridge University Press.

Newmeyer, F. J. (1986). *The politics of linguistics.* Chicago: The University of Chicago Press.

Norman, R., & Sayers, S. (Eds.). (1980). *Hegel, Marx and dialectic: A debate.* Sussex, England: The Harvester Press.

Norris, C. (1990). *What's wrong with postmodernism.* Baltimore, MD: The Johns Hopkins University Press.

O'Connor, N. (1966). *Present-day Russian psychology.* Oxford: Pergamon Press.

Oller, J. W., Jr. (1973). Some psycholinguistic controversies. In J. Oller et al. (Eds.), *Focus on the learner: Pragmatic perspectives for the language teacher.* Rowley, MA: Newbury House Publishers.

Oller, J., & Richards, J. C. (Eds.). (1973). *Focus on the learner: Pragmatic perspectives for the language teacher.* Rowley, MA: Newbury House Publishers.

Otero, C. P. (Ed.). (1988). *Noam Chomsky: Language and politics.* Montreal: Black Rose Books.

Payne, T. R. (1968). *S. L. Rubinštejn and the philosophical foundations of Soviet psychology.* Dordrecht, Holland: D. Reidel Publishing Company.

Pribram, K. H. (1996). Of Russians and Russia. In Vera A. Koltsova et al. (Eds.), *Post-Soviet perspectives on Russian psychology.* Westport, CT: Greenwood Press.

Průcha, J. (1972). *Soviet psycholinguistics.* The Hague: Mouton.

Průcha, J. (Ed.). (1976). *Soviet studies in language and language behavior.* Amsterdam: North-Holland Publishing Company.

Rahmani, L. (1973). *Soviet psychological: Philosophical, theoretical, and experimental issues.* New York: International Universities Press.

Ratner, C. (1991). *Vygotsky's sociohistorical psychology and its contemporary applications.* New York: Plenum Press.

Rauch, I. (1980). Distinguishing semiotics from linguistics and the position of language in both. In Bailey (Ed.), *The sign: semiotics around the world* (pp. 328–334). Ann Arbor: Michigan Slavic Publications. New York: Oxford University Press.

Resnick, L. (1994). Situated rationalism: Biological and social preparation for learning. In Hirschfield et al. (Eds.), *Mapping the mind: domain specificity in cognition and culture.* New York: Cambridge University Press.

Richards, M. P. M. (Ed.). (1974). *The integration of the child into a social world.* Cambridge, England: Cambridge University Press.

Rieber, R. (Ed.). (1987). *The collected works of L. S. Vygotsky.* Vol. 1. New York: Plenum Press.

Rieber, R. (Ed.). (1997). *The collected works of L. S. Vygotsky.* Vol. 4: *The history of the development of higher mental functions.* New York: Plenum Press.

Rieber, R. (1999). *The Collected Works of L. S. Vygotsky.* Vol. 6: *Scientific legacy.* New York: Kluwer Academic/Plenum Publishers.

Rieber, R., & Wollock, J. (Eds.). (1997). *The collected works of L. S. Vygotsky.* Vol. 3: *Problems of the theory and history of psychology.* trans. R. van der Veer. New York: Plenum Press.

Rissom, I. (1985). *Der Begriff des Zeichens in den Arbeiten Lev Semenovic Vygotskijs.* (The concept of sign in the works of Lev Semonovich Vygotsky). Göppingen, Germany: Kümmerle Verlag.

Rivers, W. (1964). *The psychologist and the foreign-language teacher.* Chicago: The University of Chicago Press.

Rivers, W. (1983). *Communicating naturally in a second language.* Cambridge, England: Cambridge University Press.

Rivers, W. (1990). Mental representations and language in action. *Georgetown University Round Table on Languages and Linguistics.* James E. Alatis, (Ed.), Washington, D.C.: Georgetown University Press.

Robbins, D. (1999). Prologue. In R. Rieber (Ed.), *The Collected Works of L. S. Vygotsky.* Vol. 6: Scientific legacy (pp. v–xii). New York: Kluwer Academic/Plenum Publishers.

Rosa, A., & Montero, I. (1992). The historical context of Vygotsky's work: A sociohistorical approach. In L. Moll (Ed.), *Vygotsky and education: Instructional implications and applications of sociohistorical psychology* (pp. 59–88). Cambridge, England: Cambridge University Press.

Roter, A. (1987). The concept of consciousness: Vygotsky's contribution. *The Quarterly Newsletter of the Laboratory of Comparative Human Cognition.* July, *9*, 105–110.

Roth, L. (1923). Spinoza and Cartesianism (I), (II). *Mind, XXXII,* 12–303.

Runes, D. D. (Ed.). (1960). *Dictionary of philosophy.* New York: Philosophical Library.

Ryan, J. (1974). Early language development. In M. P. M. Richards (Ed.), *The integration of the child into a social world.* Cambridge, England: Cambridge University Press.

Rzhevsky, N. (1994). Kozhinov on Bakhtin. *New Literary History, 25,* 429–444.

Saporta, S. (1961). *Psycholinguistics: A book of readings.* New York: Holt, Rinehart and Winston.

Sartre, J.-P. (1976). *Critique of dialectical reason: Theory of practical ensembles.* trans. A. Sheridan-Smith. J. Dee (Ed.). London: Humanities Press.

Schwartz, R. (1969). On knowing a grammar. In S. Hook (Ed.), *Language and philosophy symposium* (pp. 183–190). New York: New York University Press.

Schwebel, M., Maher, C. A., & Fagley, N. S. (Eds.). (1990). *Promoting cognitive growth over the life span*. Hillsdale, NJ: Lawrence Erlbaum Associates.

Scribner, S. (1985). Vygotsky's uses of history. In J. V. Wertsch (Ed.), *Culture, communication, and cognition* (pp. 119–145). Cambridge, England: Cambridge University Press.

Scribner, S. (1997). Vygotsky's uses of history. In E. Tobach (Ed.), *Mind and social practice: Selected writings of Sylvia Scribner* (pp. 241–265). Cambridge, England: Cambridge University Press.

Sebeok, T. A. (Ed.). (1968). *Current trends in linguistics: Vol. 1 Soviet and East European linguistics*. The Hague: Mouton.

Silverstein, M. (1987). The three faces of "function": Preliminaries to a psychology of language. In M. Hickman (Ed.), *Social and functional approaches to language and thought*. Orlando, FL: Academic Press.

Simon, B. (Ed.). (1957). *Psychology in the Soviet Union*. Stanford, CA: Stanford University Press.

Sinclair, H. (1972). Some comments of Fodor's' reflections on L. S. Vygotsky's Thought and language. *Cognition, 1*.

Sinha, C. (1988). *Language and representation*. New York: Harvester Press.

Slama-Cazacu, T. (1983). Theoretical prerequisites for a contemporary applied linguistics. In B. Bain (Ed.), *The sociogenesis of language and human conduct* (pp. 257–271). New York: Plenum Press.

Smirnov, S. D. (1981–82). The world of images and the image of the world. *Soviet Psychology, 20,* 3–27.

Sobkin, V. S., & Leontiev, D. A. (1992). The beginning of a new psychology: Vygotsky's psychology of art. In G. C. Cupchik et al. (Eds.), *Emerging visions of the aesthetic process: Psychology, semiology, and philosophy*. Cambridge, England: Cambridge University Press.

Sokolov, A. N. (1972). *Inner speech and thought*. New York: Plenum Press.

Spinoza, B. (1955) [1766]. *On the improvement of the understanding. The Ethics. Correspondence*. Mineola: Dover Publications.

Steffe, L. P., & Gale, J. (Eds.). (1995). *Constructivism in education*. Hillsdale, NJ: Lawrence Erlbaum Associates.

Steiner, P. (1981). In defense of semiotics: The dual asymmetry of cultural signs. *New Literary History,* 416–135.

Steiner, P. (Ed.). (1982). *The Prague school: Selected writings, 1929–1946*. Austin: University of Texas Press.

Stetsenko, A. P. (1989). World image and the ontogeny of consciousness. *Soviet Psychology, 27,* 6–25.

Talyzina, N. (1961). *The psychology of learning*. Moscow: Progress Publishers.

Tharp, R. G., & Gallimore, R. (1988). *Rousing minds to life*. Cambridge, England: Cambridge University Press.

Tihanov, G. (1998). Vološinov, ideology, and language: The birth of Marxist sociology from the spirit of *Lebensphilosophie*. *The South Atlantic Quarterly, 97,* 599–622.

Tobach, E. (Ed.). (1997). *Mind and social practice: Selected writings of Sylvia Scribner.* Cambridge, England: Cambridge University Press.

Tul'viste, P. (1989a). Discussion of the works of L. S. Vygotsky in the USA, *Soviet Psychology, 27,* 37–52.

Tul'viste, P. (1989b). Education and the development of concepts: Interpreting results of experiments with adults with and without schooling. *Soviet Psychology, 27,* 5–21.

Tulviste, P. (1991). *The cultural–historical development of verbal thinking*. trans. M. Jaroszewska Hall. Commack, NY: Nova Science Publishers.

Umrikhin, V. (1997). Russian and world psychology: A common origin of divergent paths. In Elena L. Grigorenko (Ed.), et al., *Psychology of Russia: Past, present, future* (pp. 17–38). Commack, N.Y.: Nova Science Publishers, Inc.

Uznadze, D. (1966). *Psikhologicheskie issledovaniya* (Psychological Investigations). Moscow: Nauka. (original paper published in German in 1929).

Valsiner, J. (1987). *Culture and the development of children's action: A cultural–historical theory of developmental psychology.* New York: John Wiley and Sons.

Valsiner, J. (1988a). *Child development within cultural structured environments. Vol. 1. Parental cognition and adult-child interaction.* Norwood, NJ: Ablex Publishing Corporation.

Valsiner, J. (1988b). *Developmental psychology in the Soviet Union.* Brighton, England: The Harvester Press.

Valsiner, J. (1996). Development, methodology, and recurrence of unsolved problems: On the modernity of "old" ideas. *Swiss Journal of Psychology, 55,* 119–125.

van der Veer, R. (1991). The anthropological underpinning of Vygotsky's thinking. *Studies in Soviet Thought, 42,* 73–91.

van der Veer, R. (1997). Some major themes in Vygotsky's theoretical work: An introduction. In R. Rieber et al. (Eds.), *The collected works of L. S. Vygotsky. Vol. 3. Problems of the theory and history of psychology,* New York: Plenum Press.

van der Veer, R., & Valsiner, J. (1988). Lev Vygotsky and Pierre Janet: On the origin of the concept of sociogenesis. *Developmental Review, 8,* 52–65.

van der Veer, R., & Valsiner, J. (1991). *Understanding Vygotsky: A quest for synthesis.* Oxford, England: Blackwell.

van der Veer, R., & Valsiner, J. (1993). The encoding of distance: The concept of zone of proximal development and its interpretations. In R. R. Cocking (Ed.), *The development and meaning of psychological distance.* Hillsdale, N.J.: Lawrence Erlbaum Associates.

van der Veer, R., & Valsiner, J. (1994). *The Vygotsky reader.* Oxford: Blackwell.

van der Veer, R., & van Ijzendoorn, M. H. (1985). Vygotksy's theory of the higher psychological processes: Some criticisms. *Human Development, 28,* 1–9.

van der Veer, R., van Ijzendoorn, M., & Valsiner, J. (Eds.). (1994). *Reconstructing the mind: Replicability in research on human development.* Norwood, N.J.: Ablex Publishing Corporation.

van Lier, L. (1996a, August). From input to affordance: Social–interactive learning from an ecological perspective. Paper given at AILA Congress, Jyväskylä, Finland.

van Lier, L. (1996b). *Interaction in the language curriculum: Awareness, autonomy & authenticity.* London: Longman.

Vari-Szilagyi, I. (1991). G. H. Mead and L. S. Vygotsky on action. *Studies in Soviet Thought, 42,* 93–122.

Vesey, G. N. A. (1964). *Body and mind.* London: George Allen and Unwin Ltd.

Vigotsky, L. S. (1961). Thought and speech. In S. Saporta (Ed.), *Psycholinguistics: A book of readings* (pp. 509–537). New York: Holt, Rinehart and Winston.

Vocate, D. (1987). *The theory of A. R. Luria.* Hillsdale, NJ: Lawrence Erlbaum Associates.

Vološinov, V. N. (1986). *Marxism and the philosophy of language.* Cambridge, MA: Harvard University Press.

Vygodskaia, G. L. (1995). Remembering father. *Educational Psychologist, 30,* 57–59.

Vygodskaia, G. L. (1996). *Lev Semonovich Vygotsky: Life, Accomplishments—Brushstrokes of a Portrait* (Written in Russian). Moscow: Academia.

Vygotsky, L. S. (1929). The problem of the cultural development of the child. *Journal of Genetic Psychology, 36,* 415–434.

Vygotsky, L. S. (1962). *Thought and language.* Ed. and trans. G. Hanfmann and G. Vakar. Cambridge, MA: M.I.T. Press.

Vygotsky, L. S. (1971) [1925]. *The psychology of art.* Cambridge, MA: M.I.T. Press.

Vygotsky, L. S. (1977). The development of higher psychological functions. *Soviet Psychology,* Spring, 60–73.

Vygotsky, L. S. (1978). *Mind in society.* Cambridge, MA: Harvard University Press.

Vygotsky, L. S. (1979a). Consciousness as a problem in the psychology of behavior. *Soviet Psychology, XVII*, 3–35.

Vygotsky, L. S. (1979b). Development of higher forms of attention. *Soviet Psychology, XVIII*, 67–115.

Vygotsky, L. S. (1981). The genesis of higher mental functions. In J. V. Wertsch (Ed.), *The concept of activity in Soviet psychology* (pp. 144–188). Armonk, NY: M.E. Sharpe.

Vygotsky, L. S. (1983). From the notebooks of L. S. Vygotsky. *Soviet Psychology, XXI*, 3–17.

Vygotsky, L. S. (1987). Emotions and their development in childhood. In R. Rieber (Ed.), *The collected works of L. S. Vygotsky*. Vol. 1 (pp. 325–337). New York: Plenum Press.

Vygotsky, L. S. (1989). [Concrete human psychology]. *Soviet Psychology, 27*, 53–77.

Vygotsky, L. S. (1990). Imagination and creativity in childhood. *Soviet Psychology, 28*, 84–96.

Vygotsky, L. (1994a). *Thought and language*. In A. Kozulin (Ed.), *Language and thought*. Cambridge, MA: M.I.T. Press.

Vygotsky, L. (1994b). Thought in schizophrenia. In R. van der Veer et al. (Eds.), *The Vygotsky reader*. Oxford: Blackwell.

Vygotsky, L. S. (1994c). The problem of the environment. In R. van der Veer et al. (Eds.), *The Vygotsky reader* (pp. 338–354). Oxford: Blackwell.

Vygotsky, L. S. (1997). *Educational psychology* trans R. Silverman. Boca Raton, FL: St. Lucie Press.

Vygotsky, L. S., & Luria, A. R. (1992). *Ape, primitive man, and child: Essays in the history of behavior*. trans. E. Rossiter. New York: Harvester-Wheatsheaf.

Vygotsky, L. S., & Luria, A. (1994). Tool and symbol in child development. In R. van der Veer et al. (Eds.), *The Vygotsky reader* (pp. 99–174). Oxford: Blackwell.

Wardekker, Willem L. (1996). Critical and Vygotskian theories of education: A comparison. Worldwide Web: March 23. address: http://www.glas.apc.org/~vega/vygodsky/wardekkr.html

Wartofsky, M. W. (1979). *Models: Representation and the scientific understanding*. Dordrecht, Holland: D. Reidel Publishing Company.

Watson, J. B. (1966 [1928]). The unconscious of the behaviorist. In E. S. Dummer (Ed.), *The unconscious: A symposium*. Freeport, NY: Books for Libraries Press.

Watson, E. (1995). What a Vygotskian perspective can contribute to contemporary philosophy of language. In D. Bakhurst et al. (Eds.), *The social self* (pp. 47–66). London: Sage Publications.

Weinreich, U. (1968). Lexicology. In T. A. Sebeok (Ed.), *Current trends in linguistics. Vol. 1* (pp. 60–93). The Hague: Mouton.

Weiskrantz, L. (Ed.). *Thought without language*. Oxford: Clarendon Press.

Wertsch, J. V. (1978). *Recent trends in Soviet psycholinguistics*. Armonk, NY: M.E. Sharpe.

Wertsch, J. V. (1980). The significance of dialogue in Vygotsky's account of social, egocentric, and inner speech. *Contemporary Educational Psychology, 5*, 150–162.

Wertsch, J. V. (1981). *The concept of activity in Soviet psychology*. Armonk, NY: M.E. Sharpe.

Wertsch, J. V. (1983). Role of semiosis in Vygotsky's theory. In B. Bain (Ed.), *The sociogenesis of language and human conduct*. New York: Plenum Press.

Wertsch, J. V. (1985a). *Culture, communication, and cognition*. Cambridge, England: Cambridge University Press.

Wertsch, J. V. (1985b). *Vygotsky and the social formation of mind*. Cambridge, MA: Harvard University Press.

Wertsch, J. V. (1988). L. S. Vygotsky's "new" theory of mind. *The American Scholar*, Winter, 81–89.

Wertsch, J. V. (1990). Dialogue and dialogism in a socio-cultural approach to mind. In I. Markovà et al. (Eds.), *The dynamics of dialogue*. New York: Harvester-Wheatsheaf Press.

Wertsch, J. V. (1991). *Voices of the mind*. Cambridge, MA: Harvard University Press.

Wertsch, J. V. (1992). The voice of rationality in a sociocultural approach to mind. In L. Moll (Ed.), *Vygotsky and education: Instructional implications and applications of sociohistorical psychology* (pp. 111–126). Cambridge, England: Cambridge University Press.

Wertsch, J. V. (1995a). Sociocultural research in the copyright age. *Culture & Psychology, 1,* 81–102.

Wertsch, J. V. (1995b). Vygotsky: The ambivalent enlightenment rationalist. In M. Cole (Ed.), *From Moscow to the fifth dimension: An exploration in romantic* science. Worchester, MA: Clark University Press.

Wertsch, J. V. (1998). *Mind as mediated action.* New York: Oxford University Press.

Wertsch, J. V., & Addison Stone, C. (1985). The concept of internalization in Vygotsky's account of the genesis of higher mental functions. In J. V. Wertsch (Ed.), *Culture, communication, and cognition* (pp. 162–179). Cambridge, England: Cambridge University Press.

Wertsch, J. V., & Bivens, J. A. (1993). The social origins of individual mental functioning: Alternatives and perspectives. In R. R. Cocking (Ed.), *The development and meaning of psychological distance* (pp. 203–218). Hillsdale, N.J.: Lawrence Erlbaum Associates.

Wertsch, J. V., & Minick, N. (1990). Negotiating sense in the zone of proximal development. In M. Schwebel et al. (Eds.), *Promoting cognitive growth over the life span* (pp. 71–88). Hillsdale, NJ: Lawrence Erlbaum Associates.

Wertsch, J. V., & Tulviste, P. (1992). L. S. Vygotsky and contemporary developmental psychology. *Developmental Psychology, 28,* 548–557.

Wertsch, J. V., del Río, P., & Alvarez, A. (Eds.). (1995). *Sociocultural studies of mind.* Cambridge, England: Cambridge University Press.

Widdowson, H. G. (1990). *Aspects of language teaching.* Oxford: Oxford University Press.

Yaroshevsky, M. G. (1999). Epilogue. In R. W. Rieber (Ed.), *The collected works of L. S. Vygotsky, Vol. 6: Scientific legacy* (pp. 245–266). New York: Kluwer Academic/Plenum Publishers.

Zimmerman, M. (1969). Is linguistic rationalism a rational linguistics? In Hook: 198–207.

Zinchenko, V. P. (1985a). Cultural–historical psychology and the psychological theory of activity: Retrospect and prospect. In J. V. Wertsch et al. (Eds.), *Culture, communication, and cognition* (pp. 37–55). Cambridge, England: Cambridge University Press.

Zinchenko, V. P. (1985b). Vygotsky's ideas about units for the analysis of mind. In J. V. Wertsch (Ed.), *Culture, communication, and cognition* (pp. 4–118). Cambridge, England: Cambridge University Press.

Zinkin, N. I. (1976). Thought and speech. In J. Průcha (Ed.), *Soviet studies in language and language behavior.* Amsterdam: North-Holland Publishing Company.

Zivan, G. (1979). *The development of self-regulation through private speech.* New York: John Wiley & Sons.

Index